THE
DUCK HUNTER'S
BIBLE

Erwin A. Bauer

THE DUCK HUNTER'S BIBLE

DOUBLEDAY & COMPANY, INC., GARDEN CITY, NEW YORK

Library of Congress Catalog Card Number 65-15543
Copyright © 1965 by Erwin A. Bauer
All Rights Reserved
Printed in the United States of America
9 8 7 6 5 4 3

Contents

THE
DUCK HUNTER'S
BIBLE

THE WONDERFUL WORLD OF WATERFOWLERS

Late in the afternoon a soft rain began to fall. Before night it would probably turn to sleet and then to snow. But now Bill Browning and I huddled beside a bend of Red Rock Creek and listened to the patter of rain on the old sheet of canvas which covered us. I shivered.

"We shouldn't have long to wait now," Bill whispered.

Some might say that only a pair of madmen would waste away a late autumn evening in Montana beside a brook formed from snows melting in the mountains. But duck hunters would understand because we were duck hunting. The evening before, Bill had watched flight after flight of mallards funnel into this place from all around, and he figured they would return. So we were waiting.

While we waited the weather changed from bad to much, much worse. First the rain became sleet and a cold vapor came pouring over the Lima Peaks of the Rockies to the west. The vapor quickly spilled into the valley—Centennial Valley—and enveloped it so thoroughly that we seemed to be suspended in a void. We might have been on another planet, so strange did it seem.

I wiggled toes inside my hip boots to try to restore circulation, and held my hands under my armpits to try to warm stiff fingers. The sleet began to freeze on the canvas. Bill shifted and pulled fur ear flaps down over his ears. That's when the first ducks came.

Eight, maybe nine mallards buzzed in so low they almost skimmed the canvas under which we crouched and then braked to a sudden, noisy landing in the creek not thirty feet away. In the next instant they were gabbling softly and nibbling on the green watercress that grew lush along both fringes of the creek. They didn't suspect danger was watching them at close range.

"Now," Bill said.

Together we threw back the canvas and jumped to our feet. For an instant time passed in slow motion; the ducks couldn't believe what they saw and they only looked at the impossible spectacle of two humans on this soggy bank. Then a hen squawked in alarm and Red Rock Creek exploded.

Maybe someone else can explain why only one drake dropped after five shots—three from Bill's pump, two from my double—were fired at relatively easy, flushing targets. But that was the score. We looked at each other sheepishly, laughed out loud and crawled back under the canvas.

"I hope that wasn't the only flight," Bill said, "or we will have more of your uninspired stew instead of duck for dinner tonight."

My waterfowling friend needn't have worried, because what followed was a waterfowler's dream of paradise suddenly come true. Mallards began pouring into that pool as if it were the last place on earth to find open water on which to spend the night. They came as singles and

doubles, by the dozens and by long irregular strings. We shot until we had a limit apiece, unloaded the shotguns and then just watched the remarkable performance until it was too dark to see any longer.

Because of the overcast, the ducks came in low, just above the ground. There seemed to be no end to them. Several times they practically brushed the canvas with their wings. Others just materialized out of nowhere. Some kind of natural radar guided them. This is something, I kept thinking, that should happen to every duck hunter on earth. It was certainly an incident I would never forget.

But to tell the truth, the sport of duck hunting is a *series* of events a man will never forget.

The wonderful world of duck hunters is something special and something different. It isn't the same as the trout fisherman's world because trout fishing is more contemplative and is associated more often with pleasant weather. Nor is duck hunting as grueling and tense as typical big-game hunting or big-game fishing can be. But it has some elements of all of these plus escape, tradition, suspense and a tremendous uncertainty.

Duck hunting gives a man a chance to see the loneliest places. Non duck hunters, who wouldn't understand, might call these the unfriendliest places. I mean blinds washed by a rolling surf, blue and gold autumn marshes, a northern bay with ice forming on the perimeter, a rice field in the rain, flooded pin-oak forests or any remote river delta. In duck hunting the scene is as important as the shooting; at least it is for me.

The scene might even be completely unreal. My best example recalls an evening not long ago in Baja California. Glenn Lau and I were sitting together beneath a thornbush on a narrow finger of gravel beach. The beach separated the salty Sea of Cortes, near Loreto, from a murky green, brackish lagoon.

We came here in the first place to collect enough whitewing doves to broil for dinner, but that plan soon changed. Instead of doves, small flights of bluewing teal and black brant kept buzzing into the lagoon. That in itself isn't so unusual, but nearly all of Baja is a sun-baked desert and the waterfowl came bursting in to us out of an incredible desert sunset. It was one weird duck-hunting scene never reproduced on

The wonderful world of duck hunters is composed of scenes like these.

(1) Sunrise on the arctic grasslands along Hudson Bay; the birds are blue geese.

(2) Sunset in central Ohio; the hunter has a limit of blacks as others pass overhead.

(3) An antique clock awakens hunters in an old duck club.

(4) Sunset on a goose refuge in Maryland; some geese are filtering back after feeding in grainfields nearby.

Sometimes waterfowling is hard work. Here author crawls on belly to get within range of cornfield geese—and this time scores.

calendars or postcards. But we had the kind of shooting nobody ever forgets.

A day in a duck blind can make serious hunters—even addicts—out of otherwise normal outdoorsmen. This is a sport in which, for the best results, you get up long before daybreak and remain out in the elements when they are the worst. There are duck hunters who will disagree, but on the average, shooting is best when the weather is least pleasant.

The influence of duck hunting on men is also evident in the great amount of money spent every year to pursue the sport. Today most of the very best waterfowl-hunting areas are leased or owned outright by duck-hunting clubs. Some of these amount to no more than the legal papers which describe the lease or ownership. But far more are fairly elaborate clubs and many border on the luxurious.

Depending on how elaborate the establishment, membership in a duck-hunting club can be downright expensive. Besides the club buildings, a number of boats, guides, dogs, decoys, food and bar supplies are necessary. In many cases there is also the matter of constant maintenance of dikes, channels and water levels with heavy equipment. Obviously the expense is great.

But so are the rewards great. A day in a duck marsh means much to many men and the cost isn't the greatest consequence. Recently an official of an automobile company told the writer that the ducks he bagged one season cost him $1238.98 per pound of meat. But it was worth it.

"You see," he explained, "I live ten days a week during duck season."

But the intention here is to state that not all waterfowling is expensive, as we shall see later on. Some sportsmen with little to spend also live ten days a week during duck season. As in fishing for sophisticated trout, this is a sport which can put a man's ingenuity to great test. If he is a clever hunter and willing at times to labor—even to sweat and to suffer—at the game, he can enjoy duck hunting that money alone cannot buy.

Duck hunting has an added fascination because it can become a year-round source of interest and activity. In few other sports is a dog a more valuable ally. And to get the most out of a duck dog—a retriever—is to spend time all through the year in training and conditioning the animal.

One duck hunter who squeezes more out of the sport than anybody I know is my neighbor and foul-weather friend Frank Sayers. I say foul weather because we invariably get bad weather when we go hunting together (which fortunately is often). Anyway, Frank built his own duck boat and decoys during the off-season, annually builds his own blinds and has trained his own Labrador (from a puppy) to be a first-class duck dog.

You could safely say Frank is the Compleat Waterfowler. I have been with Frank when the shooting was very good and when it was very bad; he has fun in either case. He has also suffered. Several years ago we were jump-shooting on Big Walnut Creek, which isn't far from where we live in central Ohio. With us was a big Lab male, Blackie, borrowed from a friend. It was the tag end of the season and most of the creek had frozen over, with only scattered areas around riffles containing open water. In these spots the blacks and mallards, plus a scattering of goldeneyes, were concentrated.

We made a classic stalk on one riffle and neatly folded up a black on the flush. The duck fell in open water and instantly Blackie plunged into the icy water and grabbed the duck. But that's when complications began.

Blackie couldn't get back on shore because he couldn't claw his way back onto the ice sheet which surrounded the open water. To tell the truth, the dog was in bad trouble. But not for too long.

Frank stripped off his pants and boots and without hesitation broke his way through the ice to belly-deep water. There he grabbed the Lab by the loose skin on the neck and dragged him out onto shore. Ice froze on both of them.

When we were finally able to thaw out Frank and the dog with the car heater, Frank's first comment was: "Did you notice that Blackie held onto the duck through the whole thing?"

I had noticed. I had also noticed other good examples of how waterfowling makes addicts of men *and* their dogs.

But how about the ducks—the targets of this book? Altogether there are 247 different kinds of ducks, geese and swans living somewhere on the face of the earth. They range in size from the tiny (less than a pound) Indian pygmy goose to the huge magpie goose of Australia and the trumpeter swan of North America. Some ducks

verge on extinction, others seem to be prospering. The Labrador duck is gone forever and the Laysan teal of the Pacific number only about thirty individuals. But in southern Argentina and New Zealand professional hunters are employed to shoot geese wholesale because they are a nuisance to agriculture.

Some species of ducks and geese must also be considered among the most beautiful birds in the world. Most American shooters are familiar with our exquisite native wood duck. But the woody has plenty of competition in the good-looks department from such as the mandarin duck and Baikal teal of Asia, from the red-crested pochard and from the Siberian red-breasted goose. The last is an aristocrat among all birds.

Some ducks live more in trees than on the water and others are only found in high torrential rivers of the Andes Mountains. Some prefer steaming jungle, while close cousins never leave arctic barrens. Some are shy and furtive; others, like the Cape Barren goose, may attack anything of any size anytime. Altogether the world's waterfowl comprise a highly interesting and exciting family of birds. It is only a shame that the future for all of them is not more bright.

Of the 247 world waterfowl, about 44 live or visit in North America occasionally. For the sake of describing them in this book, we will divide them into four groups: large puddle ducks, small puddle ducks, diving ducks, geese and brant. A separate chapter is devoted to each group.

Puddle ducks are typically birds of fresh, shallow marshes and rivers rather than large lakes and bays. However, this is not a hard-and-fast statement of habitat. They are good divers, but ordinarily feed by dabbling or tipping rather than by completely submerging.

By contrast diving ducks frequent larger, deeper lakes and rivers, coastal bays and inlets. Nor is this a hard-and-fast statement. The divers are usually grouped together because they do feed most often by submerging, often to considerable depths.

Ten kinds of geese or brant and three kinds of swans may be encountered by American waterfowlers. Two of the swans (the trumpeter and whistler) are native, and the third (the mute swan) from the Old World is now semi-wild in places. But hunting the swans, once done for the market, is no longer permitted.

Mallard comes in for landing on small pothole—and hunter rises up and hits bird. Notice that the dog is already on the way to retrieve.

A wise and serious duck hunter can expand both the "hunting" season and his own pleasure by becoming an expert in waterfowl identification. In these days when seasons are either restricted or closed on many species, identification is doubly important. Identifying waterfowl can give many hours of satisfying recreation, and if you carry a camera in place of a gun, the hunting season is never closed. There's also a possible dividend in capturing live action and rare beauty on film.

When redheads or canvasbacks or any other species are protected because of their scarcity, it is essential that a hunter identify the target before he pulls the trigger. But a cameraman "fires" and bothers about the species later.

Knowing a mallard from a merganser has another side, too. Try cooking both at the same time and in the same manner and see which is delicious and which actually isn't fit to eat.

Let's digress a moment and see exactly what is involved in identifying ducks and geese. You can look for color and pattern of plumage, of course, and if the ducks are near enough and not in motion this is a good way. But knowing plumage and color isn't enough. Besides, many ducks wear different plumage in summer, called eclipse plumage, than they do in spring and fall. This accounts for such confusion as hunters identifying male ducks as females early in the hunting season. Often during this period drakes haven't had time to regain their "normal" plumage after the summertime molt.

There are other factors which confuse identification. Adult birds are likely to vary slightly from immature birds. And even chemical or mineral content of water can change a duck's color. White-breasted ducks, for example, may show up as yellow or brown after lengthy exposure to a mineral-laden pond.

The complete duck hunter does not rely on plumage alone to guide him. Instead he checks the habitat, the action or behavior, the shape or silhouette, and the voice of the bird. Some birds can be positively identified by voice—the woody, for one example. Others, such as the drake pintail, can be positively identified by shape no matter what the stage of his plumage.

The antics and maneuvers of a flock of waterfowl in the air can help indicate many species. Mallards, pintails and widgeons form loose

Success. Hunter holds up a Canada goose shot from a pit blind he built himself on a lonely Lake Erie island.

groups. Sometimes the individual birds in a flock seem to be going in all directions at once although aiming at the same place. Teal and shovelers flash past in small, marvelously coordinated groups. Fire at them or startle them and the groups seem to explode, regrouping again later on.

Mergansers often appear in single file. Canvasbacks change from wavy lines to irregular V's and back again. Redheads "boil up" in short flights from one end of a lake to another. You get the impression they are very nervous.

A good observer can often identify ducks from wingbeats, because some are only fast and others are very, very fast. Some fly with short, rapid fluttering of the wings; others take long strokes. Even the sound of wings can be important. Canvasbacks zoom past with a steady "rush" of wings, while the pinions of goldeneyes whistle during flight. All these things become evident with experience and it's highly rewarding experience, too.

There are few dull moments in the wonderful world of duck hunters. Any duck hunt can be high adventure. The adventure may come in the form of a sudden, savage blizzard or in the precarious punt-boat ride across a choppy bay from freezing blind to cozy clubhouse. It can come when a peregrine falcon dives down in to the decoys and almost turns inside out when, too late, it discovers its mistake. The adventure may be when a rare species is bagged or when the dog makes a spectacular retrieve of a cripple. And it may even happen when an angry mother hippopotamus chases you from your makeshift blind beside a Tanganyika water hole. That actually happened to me.

Like Frank Sayers and millions of other addicted waterfowlers, I really do live ten days a week during open season.

Chapter 1

LARGE PUDDLE DUCKS

Distributed about the earth are ninety-eight forms of river and pond ducks, also called surface-feeding or puddle ducks. Sixteen of these are seen in North America if the transient European widgeon and European teal are included. A number of specific characteristics separate these puddle ducks from the diving ducks and fish ducks also found in North America.

These characteristics are as follows: (1) In flushing from land or water, puddle ducks do so with a strong vertical upward motion as if being catapulated skyward. Most other ducks, on the other hand, patter or "run" along the surface for some distance before take-off.

(2) Pond ducks ordinarily feed in shallow water by tipping up (with head under water) or by dabbling along the fringes of relatively small bodies of water. Their diet consists largely of vegetable matter and they rarely dive, except when injured to escape danger. On the whole, puddle ducks are better ducks on the table than any others.

(3) Legs of the puddle ducks are placed somewhat nearer the middle of the body than in other waterfowl and therefore they are able to move about more freely on land than are the diving ducks and mergansers (fish-eating ducks). Also, the hind toe of puddle ducks is smaller and less noticeable than it is on diving ducks.

(4) The colored patch on the secondary flight feathers of the wings of puddle ducks, called the speculum, is usually more highly colored and iridescent than it is on diving ducks.

(5) Puddle ducks and divers differ from the mergansers in that their bills are broad and flat, whereas mergansers have narrow and nearly cylindrical bills which are saw-toothed.

Whenever ducks are observed feeding in grainfields, crop fields or almost anywhere on land, more than likely they will be puddle ducks. They are partial to ripened grain, and as we mentioned before, most of this group are sure-footed and can walk or even run well on land. Any ducks found feeding in woods or forests are almost certain to be puddle ducks. Mallards or wood ducks fattened on acorns are among the most highly regarded food ducks of all.

The Common Mallard

Among all the ducks on earth, the common mallard is probably the most abundant. This species lives and nests throughout the entire Northern Hemisphere. On our own continent it is somewhat more abundant in the western portion because its place is filled in the east (somewhat) by the black duck, a close relative.

Besides being the most abundant duck, the mallard has been of greatest importance to man as well. It readily becomes domesticated and nearly all of today's domestic breeds of ducks originated in the mallard. In many parts of Asia both the meat and the eggs of mallards are an important part of the food supply.

Even after the turn of the century and up until World War I, mallards were an important source of food in the United States. Market hunters pursued them everywhere. During one season at Big Lake, Arkansas, a single gunner shot 8000 mallards and sold them on the market.

A mallard drake, the most popular and among the most handsome of American waterfowl. This fellow is fast on the wing and great on the table. (PHOTO KARL H. MASLOWSKI)

That is only a fraction of the 120,000 sent to market from this same general area in that one year. Today, however, all that is changed, and as this is written, the limit is two mallards per day per hunter in the Mississippi flyway. Let's hope it falls no lower.

In many ways the mallard is every sportsman's duck. It may not be the fastest among our waterfowl on the wing, but it is extremely fast. It is also among the largest and most handsome of our native ducks and surely it is one of the best on the table. Because it decoys well, but not *too* well, it is certainly the most sought after of all ducks. A handsome male greenhead, appropriately named for its rich iridescent green head which shows a purplish gloss in sunlight, is an elegant trophy.

Unless it is an extremely dark day, mallards are not too difficult to identify in flight. When startled, mallards spring from the water and rise upward vertically for several feet before finally leveling off in flight. When under way the head and neck are carried forward and slightly upward. The body appears rather large, and the wingspread is greater than among diving ducks.

In full flight the forward and rear portions of the drake mallard appear dark, while the breast and underwings seem to be light. Most of the

How a hunter ordinarily sees mallards—deployed high overhead. (SOUTH CARO-
LINA WILDLIFE RESOURCES DEPT. PHOTO BY BROWN)

time the white bars of the speculum are also
evident.

The female mallard is somewhat more difficult
to identify than the male. Sometimes the white
bars of the speculum can be seen. Except for
these white wing bars, however, it is very easy
to confuse the hen mallard with the hen pintail.

Compared to other ducks, mallards are noisy
birds. They quack loudly in flight but even more
so when on the feeding grounds. The male's call
is a low quack that can be heard long distances.
The female has a loud resonant quack and this
is what shooters hear when a flock of mallards
circles around the decoys.

Mallards nest and breed most extensively in
the northwest quarter of North America. They
winter throughout the United States wherever
there is open water, with the greatest concentration in the lower half of the Mississippi Valley
and in the Gulf states from Florida to Texas.
Twice a year, in the spring and the fall, they
migrate between the summer and winter areas.

In early autumn mallards become restless. As
early as September they begin flights from local
nesting areas to nearby feeding grounds. But the
main migration flights do not begin in earnest
until late September or October. Then as the
days become golden and all vegetation changes

Mallards coming in to the decoys.

colors, mallards begin to gather in huge flocks, and on sharp, frosty nights they begin their flights southward. These are the flights which waterfowlers so eagerly await.

Depending upon their location and the situation, mallards are hunted by every conceivable legal means: by shooting from fixed blinds over decoys, by jump-shooting in rivers and ponds, by waiting in grainfields, and by pass-shooting along established lines of flight.

Mallards average slightly over two and a half pounds in weight, with drakes being heavier than females. Average wingspread is thirty-six inches.

Hunter flushing mallards from pothole in Beaverhead County, Montana. This is common way to bag mallards.

The Black Duck

If native North American ducks are ever classified for shyness, wariness and pure intelligence, the black duck would have to win most of the prizes. At least that is the consensus of most hunters in the eastern half of the United States who know them.

This handsome large duck is similar to and at least equal to the mallard in almost every way except in beauty. It is dark brown to black in color with white only underneath the wings. It is a swift flyer usually at very high altitudes and is a very delicious bird on the table. Blacks are called by many local names and perhaps we would be wise to list some of them here. For example there are black mallard, black, blackie, beef duck, brown duck, summer duck, velvet duck and, in French Canada, *canard noir*.

Generally the black is a bird of the eastern states using only the Atlantic and Mississippi fly-

Unusual photos of black ducks (with a few mallards mixed in) at rest on a northern Ohio pond. Blacks are very wary, shy birds.

ways. It is often seen in the company of mallards, but along the Atlantic seaboard it frequents salt marshes and brackish lagoons in the ocean much more than mallards. In voice, silhouette, and habits it is very similar to the mallard, although it rarely decoys as readily and is far more difficult to attract into close shotgunning range.

The main breeding and nesting areas of the black extend from the Great Lakes vicinity northeastward to Labrador and eastward to the Altantic coast. The main wintering area is in the southeastern quarter of the United States.

The first autumn flights southward begin early in September at roughly the same time bluewing teal begin to move. Then throughout the autumn the flights, composed of relatively small numbers of birds, increase in volume until late autumn, when all the birds have probably reached their wintering areas. During late autumn and winter and sometimes during the later portions of the open waterfowl seasons, blacks are forced to salt water and the sea because fresh-water ponds inland are frozen. At these periods the blacks change somewhat from a vegetable diet to an animal diet and at these times they are not so good to eat.

There is some chance to confuse the black duck with the hen mallard, but ordinarily blacks are much darker in color. On dull days they appear to be solid black and gray under the wings. In addition, the two white bars of the mallard's speculum are missing in the black duck. Hunters also confuse scoters with blacks because they have similar color and are abundant in the same general areas of the Atlantic seaboard. However, scoters have larger heads and shorter necks.

The average black duck weighs over two and a half pounds and the wingspread is about thirty-six inches for adult birds.

The American Pintail

It is difficult for most dedicated waterfowlers to discuss the pintail duck without becoming almost lyrical. It is an extremely elegant, graceful bird, both on the water and in flight. Anyone who has hunted often in pintail country has thrilled to the zigzagging maneuvers at great

heights before the birds finally level off for a landing, perhaps among the hunter's decoys. More than a few hunters have been so fascinated with this maneuver that they neglected to shoot as the birds descended.

The drake pintail is characterized by a long pointed tail, a white collar and a dark-brown head which changes from purple to pink to green in certain kinds of sunlight. By contrast, the female is a drab light brown and lacks even the pointed tail. But together they constitute one of our most abundant waterfowl species. And pintails have the widest breeding range of all our ducks.

Actually, pintails are circumpolar in distribution, with close cousins found in northern Europe and Asia. However, the main breeding range of the American pintail includes the northwest quarter of the United States and all the western half of Canada and Alaska. The forty-ninth state is an extremely important nesting area. The wintering area covers all the coastal regions of the United States, all of Mexico and Central America, and even extends into northern South America. I have seen pintails in considerable numbers on the Magdalena River of central Colombia.

On the water pintails are very nervous birds and seem always on the alert, and ready to take alarm. When surprised, they bounce vertically upward as do mallards and teals and they often bunch closely as they rise—which means they furnish an unusual target for gunners. Pintails usually approach decoys from a great height and then circle warily, as if looking for unnatural movement below. If they are satisfied that all is safe, they will plunge down quickly among the decoys. Otherwise they will turn and swiftly hurry away.

In autumn, pintails are among the early migrants. They are often found in the first bags of the season, usually with teal and locally raised mallards and black ducks. Although pintails are taken by hunters in all four major flyways, they are most abundant in the Pacific and Central flyways.

There is great difference of opinion among the most experienced duck hunters on the intelligence of pintails. Perhaps the best way to describe them is to say that they are highly erratic. On some days they seem to plunge in to

Drake pintail at rest with black ducks in background. Pintail is among the world's most graceful, attractive ducks.

Hen pintail is more drab than drake, but a great flyer and table bird. (PHOTO KARL H. MASLOWSKI)

the decoys with great abandon and without giving much thought to the matter. On other days it's practically impossible to decoy them in to even the best-placed stool. Maybe this is all to the good, because it only makes hunting of this fascinating game bird all the more interesting.

Pintail males average over two pounds each; hens go just under two pounds. The average wingspread is thirty-four inches.

Gadwall

In many ways the gadwall is a contradiction. Although it probably has a wider world distribution than any other duck, South America and Australia being the only two places where it is not found, it really isn't plentiful anywhere. In North America it is primarily a bird of the west and central regions. Inside these regions it may be reasonably plentiful in certain isolated localities and then entirely absent in localities nearby. Even though it is an easy duck to identify, it is often confused with the female pintail and the young drake pintail, with which it frequently associates.

While resting on the water, gadwalls appear as medium to fairly small gray-brown ducks on which the heads and necks seem lighter in color. At a distance and in poor light they may resemble black ducks. On the water they are more likely to be in company with other ducks, especially baldpates and pintails, than they are to be in a flock composed entirely of other gadwalls. In flight these neutral-colored birds move in small compact flocks very swiftly and usually on a direct course. The body appears to be slender as a pintail's and the wingbeat is rapid.

Since the gadwall is the only puddle duck with a white speculum on the wing, this is the mark to look for in passing birds. Remember, though, that the baldpate also has white on the wing, but it is on the forepart. Sometimes the black rump of the male gadwall will be noticeable in flight and this is another way to identify the species. While flying or on the water, drakes often make a whistling and cack-cacking noise. Hens quack in a manner similar to mallards, although it is much softer.

Of all the puddle ducks, the gadwall is the one most likely to be seen diving rather than tipping up for food. However, this is not a common occurrence. The bird walks very well and on occasion may wander far from water into grainfields and nearby woods for food.

Gadwalls breed in northwestern United States and southwestern Canada. Their wintering area is concentrated from California and the Gulf coast southward to central Mexico. Hunters are likely to see them at any time during the fall migration. However, there seems to be less regularity in their movements than in the migrations of some other ducks.

There is great disagreement on the edibility of gadwalls. All of the few I have eaten have been extremely delicious and I would rate them at least on a par with mallards and black ducks.

Male gadwalls average two pounds; females less than two pounds. Average wingspread is about thirty-three inches.

Baldpate

The baldpate is another of those ducks with many names. Among them are widgeon, American widgeon, bald-headed widgeon, northern widgeon, bald duck, French teal, gray duck, poacher duck, robber duck, whistler, and white belly. However, baldpate and widgeon are most widely used, with the former coming from the pure-white top of the head on the drakes.

It is true that many American gunners do not rate baldpates very highly. However, I have enjoyed some memorable days with them in the marshes around the western shore of Lake Erie and consider baldpates extremely fine game birds and good table birds as well. They fly swiftly in small compact flocks and in irregular formation. They seldom fly directly from one place to another but instead make twists and turns and other fancy maneuvers that make shooting on a windy day an extremely exciting proposition.

Baldpates rest nervously on the water with chest lower and tails higher than some other puddle ducks. They quickly take alarm and then jump vertically into the air, while making a rattling sound with their wings. In flight the flocks are fairly easily recognized by the conspicuous markings of the male. For example, there is the white crown on the head and the white breast. However, after spending time in certain kinds of water, I have seen baldpates with yellow and even brown breasts, discolored by the water.

Females also have white breasts, whitish wing patches, and gray underwing surfaces. This is similar to the female gadwall except that the female baldpate has no white in the speculum.

The American wildfowler on a typical day is treated to many wild and primeval sounds, such as the sigh of a northeast wind and the quacks and honkings of geese in the distance. But just as exciting is the wild and musical note of the male baldpate as it passes by a blind and carefully examines the decoys. The female's cry is much louder and also more coarse, and her quack of alarm really seems to express great terror.

Among the nicknames for the baldpate is robber duck, and I have had the rare opportunity to see how this name was earned. Through a spotting scope one day, I watched a number of baldpates mixed in among a larger number of canvasbacks and redheads. The cans and red-

Baldpate drake. The white skullcap is distinctive. (PHOTO KARL H. MASLOWSKI)

heads would dive and bring vegetation to the surface, at which point a baldpate would immediately snatch it away. Since baldpates cannot dive very deeply or very well, this is a common way of obtaining food. But by way of payment, they warn the dimmer-witted redheads and canvasbacks when danger approaches.

Early in the season baldpates come very readily to decoys. And curiosity causes younger birds especially to return again and again to look over the decoys even after hunters have fired at them in the first pass. At one time in the hickory-smoked past, market hunters reduced the number of baldpates to a dangerous level. But since market hunting and spring shooting have been abolished, the baldpate has increased and today exists in fairly good numbers.

A close relative of the baldpate is the European widgeon. It evidently reaches North America in numbers, but hunters see and bag them so rarely that it is not important enough to be considered in great detail here.

European and American widgeon are similar in size, averaging one and a half pounds each. Average wingspread is thirty-three inches.

Chapter 2

SMALL PUDDLE DUCKS

Bluewing Teal

It is unfortunate that too few American duck hunters ever become intimately acquainted with the bluewing teal. This little fellow, exclusively a resident of the New World, is remarkable any way you look at him. He is fast and among the most difficult targets among game birds of the world. He's a handsome bird too, and I believe far and away the best eating bird of all North American wildfowl.

To tell the truth, the bluewing is my favorite both on the wing and in the broiler.

If the species has a fault, it is that he is such an early migrant. The small compact flocks of bluewings leave northern nesting grounds early in September or sometimes even in August and have passed southward often before waterfowl seasons are well under way along the flyways. Occasionally if timing is right, sportsmen will have a limited amount of shooting on the first few days of the season. But usually that is all.

It is hard to describe the exciting flight of bluewings to someone who hasn't seen them perform. Small flocks, which may average from five to fifteen birds, dart swiftly, often very low over the marshes, twisting and dodging around trees and bushes. There is no predicting where they are going and when they will get there. You can hear their uniquely twittering calls in flight as they approach, and if they should pass your blind there is no guarantee that you will have birds for the pot. When a shot is fired at a passing flock, the individual birds seem to explode and dart away in all directions, but quickly re-group and continue their flight. Often enough to make it very interesting, they will swing around and pass over the blind a second or a third time. This doesn't mean that even an experienced shooter will bag enough birds for dinner.

On the water the bluewing teal appears very small in size, but size alone is not a good identifying feature because the silhouette resembles some of the larger puddle ducks. Perhaps the best distinguishing features are the blue wing patches of both sexes and the white crescent-shaped cheek markings of the male. At close range this white cheek patch is especially noticeable, as is the white patch on each flank near the base of the tail.

Unless the light is good enough to reveal the blue wing patch, the female bluewing teal is extremely difficult to distinguish from the female greenwing and the cinnamon teal. The female shoveler is also similar in appearance except for a slightly larger size and the unique bill. On the water, bluewings seldom tip up while feeding. Instead, they collect small bits of vegetation on the surface or just under the surface in water which is only a few inches deep.

Unlike many puddle ducks, bluewings are silent while feeding. But while flying, drakes utter a whistling peep that is often repeated and then a soft lisping note that at a distance may be confused with the wood duck. Females utter only a soft faint quack and this less often than the quacking of many other female ducks. When feeding, bluewings usually remain in close groups so that they almost seem to be touching one another.

Hen and drake bluewing teal, a remarkably interesting species of wildfowl. Drake is easy to identify by white mark on cheek. (PHOTO MASLOWSKI & GOOD-PASTER)

The nesting and breeding area of bluewing teal covers nearly all the plains and pothole country of the western United States and Canada. The wintering area extends from southern United States, particularly Florida and the Louisiana delta country, through Cuba, Puerto Rico, Mexico, Central America and southward far into South America. I have enjoyed excellent winter shooting for bluewing teal in Cuba and in Costa Rica, where the birds were abundant in the Guanacaste marshes.

As early as late summer in August, bluewings in the northern pothole country stir and become restless. By the end of August many of the old males fly southward, and the waterfowler who doesn't go afield for reconnaissance before opening day never even sees them. Then later in September the females and young birds of the year also begin their migration southward. Many of these birds stop briefly en route, but there is evidence that a good portion of them fly with only very brief stops before they finally arrive at their wintering grounds in warmer climates.

The speed and agility of bluewings in flight is so amazing and has astounded duck hunters so much that they have been given credit for attaining speeds of ninety to a hundred miles an hour. Of course, such speeds are vastly over-estimated, but still there is no way to accurately measure the speed. However, these tiny teal have established some amazing speed and endurance records. A teal banded in Quebec, Canada, on September 5 was killed on October 2 in British Guiana, a direct airline distance of 2400 miles from the point it was banded. This bird had flown at least eighty-five miles a day, perhaps against strong winds, for twenty-eight days to cover that distance in this length of time.

Other records have shown teal covering distances up to two hundred miles a day on shorter total flights.

I have never known a bluewing teal of any age which was not fat, juicy and tender when cooked for dinner. This includes bluewings bagged from as far north as Manitoba and northern Ohio, and as far south as Baja California and Cuba.

Greenwing Teal

Next to the wood duck, most outdoorsmen will agree that the greenwing teal is the most beautiful North American duck. When resting quietly in the sun on a calm undisturbed pond, it has been described as resembling a delicate porcelain duck.

Being the smallest of the North American ducks, the greenwing can easily be distinguished from any except the other teals and the buffleheads. Greenwings usually appear shorter in the body and have shorter necks than bluewings. But as in identifying other ducks, the size alone should never be considered as conclusive. While resting on ponds and small lakes, which are likely places to find them, greenwings seem to be much more calm and collected than some other ducks. It isn't unusual to see them loafing on sandbars, beaches or mud flats, where they often sit preening their feathers and sunning for long periods at a time, just as beautiful girls lounge beside a swimming pool.

The flight of the greenwing is very similar to that of the bluewing, fast and erratic. They have a habit of wheeling and circling together in a

Greenwing teal drake, one of world's smallest and most handsome ducks. (PHOTO KARL H. MASLOWSKI)

Hunter Glenn Lau ready to take shot at teal as it circles small lagoon in Baja California, a wintering area for the species.

as soon as deep cold and snowstorms arrive, the greenwings suddenly disappear, and the next time anyone sees them they are in warmer latitudes farther south. The greenwing's main wintering area consists of the southern third of the United States and most of the northern half of Mexico, where good shooting exists throughout the winter.

A duck of inland sloughs, marshes and slow-moving streams, the greenwing feeds by reaching down to sift food from muddy bottoms or to pluck weeds which exist in very shallow places. Characteristically it feeds by tipping up, and it is common to see this duck kicking its feet in the air to maintain its equilibrium. Among the most active ducks on land, it can run quickly, and occasionally wanders far from the water in search of such foods as berries, acorns and wild grain. On a number of occasions, while exercising my bird dogs, I have accidentally flushed greenwing teal before the season opened, far from water.

Greenwings are not very sophisticated ducks in that they decoy rather easily. Often they will make low passes time and again across a spread of decoys before finally dropping in to them. Particularly early in the season, they may rise, circle uncertainly and drop in to the decoys a second time after having been shot at previously. Roasted, baked or broiled, greenwings are just as delicious on the table as their close cousins the bluewings.

dense flock, as do domestic pigeons. During flight the wings make an audible whistling sound. As easily as the other puddle ducks, greenwings spring vertically upward for from eight to ten feet from either water or dry ground before leveling off to regular flight.

The normal breeding range of the greenwing teal extends farther north than that of the bluewing. Its center of greatest abundance is in the huge prairie areas of western Canada. The limit of the breeding range extends northward to the Arctic Circle and includes a large part of Alaska.

Fall migrations begin with the first cold weather, and in the far north that can be early in the season. But instead of hurrying southward as rapidly as the bluewings, greenwings often stop and linger wherever they find attractive feeding and where they can be undisturbed. But

Cinnamon Teal

Among all our puddle ducks, the cinnamon or red teal is the only North American species which is confined in range to the western portion of the continent. This is a familiar bird to sportsmen along the Pacific flyway and to some extent to those on the Central flyway. However, it is only an accident when encountered along the Mississippi and Atlantic flyways.

The cinnamon teal is distinct in another way in that there are two separate populations in the New World. One of these exists in western North America as described above, and the other lives in southern South America. The closest distance between the two is about two thousand miles, but as nearly as can be determined from band returns, no migrations exist between these two widely separated areas.

Cinnamon teal are birds of tule-bordered, shallow edges of lakes and marshes from Alaska southward to California. Not nearly as gregarious as other puddle ducks, they are seldom found in large flocks. Once the breeding season has passed, they are mostly encountered in pairs or family groups.

Breeding range of the cinnamon teal is pretty much confined to the western third of the United States plus a portion of British Columbia and Alberta. The winter range is that portion of the southwestern United States and Mexico just south of the breeding range. The autumn migration of cinnamon teal is really just a shift southward that begins early in September and is accomplished during that month and through October. During that shift southward, west coast gunners are furnished with considerable action.

In flight it is a difficult matter to distinguish the cinnamon teal from bluewings and greenwings, except that in good light they have a distinctly red color and they do have blue wing patches on both sexes.

Among the most trusting of North American waterfowl, cinnamon teal are often slow to take alarm. When sufficiently frightened, however, they burst into the air vertically and disappear by flying low and erratically over the marshlands. They are very silent birds, especially in flight. Occasionally the male utters a low rattling or chattering sound which never carries very far. The female has only a simple, soft quack. Cinnamon teal compare to bluewings and greenwings on the table.

Shoveler

At first close-up glance, the shoveler may seem completely unrelated to any other duck. However, it does superficially resemble the mallard. It is much smaller than the mallard and in many ways bears a close resemblance to the teal. In fact, it is closely related to teal in habit and other characteristics.

The shoveler is known by a number of other unique names worth mentioning here. Included are spoonbill, shovel duck, shovelhead, laughing mallard, scooper duck, dipper duck, mud duck, cow frog, French teal, shovelnose, spoonbill teal and broadbill.

At first the green head of the male shoveler does suggest the drake mallard. However, the large oversize bill shaped like a spatula immediately separates this bird from any other North American waterfowl. Even at a considerable distance the shoveler isn't too hard to distinguish from other puddle ducks. The male sits low on the water with his bill pointed in a downward slope. He also shows more white on his body. The female is a plain brown, as are many other ducks, but the female shoveler has the same flat head and large bill as the male. This is easy to distinguish on the water or in flight.

Mostly, shovelers are encountered in pairs or in small flocks. When startled or frightened their flight somewhat resembles that of the teal, since it is erratic and has frequent downward plunges. However, shovelers are in no way as fast flyers as any of the teals. They can rise vertically from the water with a noisy rattling of wings; they can also light almost vertically with scarcely a splash.

Shovelers are not noisy birds. They have small throats and correspondingly weak voices. The male utters a low grunting sound and the female has a feeble quack. But even these sounds are seldom heard by duck hunters.

Although not of special interest to sportsmen, the shoveler is unique in that polyandry is practiced with great regularity. In other words, the female shoveler usually has more than one mate. One is an old male and the other is a younger male, perhaps a handy combination for the gal. But what is most unique of all is that the two males seem to get along very well in this unusual situation. The reason for this unusual behavior is the fact that young females do not nest in their first season. Rather they gather together in spring and summer and live in spinsterhood until their second migration northward. As a result there are always twice as many available males of the species.

Another interesting feature about the shoveler is that some of them annually make the two-thousand-mile flight from Alaska to the Hawaiian Islands. Alaska is an important breeding area and Hawaii is an important wintering area.

Among all the puddle ducks the shoveler probably ranks lowest as a game bird. It decoys

Drake shoveler which superficially resembles a drake mallard. But spatula-shaped bill is a giveaway. (PHOTO KARL H. MASLOWSKI)

easily, maybe too easily, and most shovelers are so thin and scrawny as to be very poor on the table. Let it be known, however, that there are some exceptions to this. In many parts of their wintering area, as in Mexico where food is abundant, shovelers can grow fat and they become nearly as palatable and tender as some of the other ducks.

A main point to remember about shovelers is that they dearly love warm weather. Southward migrations begin early in September and usually are finished a month later. In springtime they wait until virtually all cold weather is finished before beginning the return trip northward. Their main habitat during the winter season is in areas where warm, shallow, inland waters are abundant.

Wood Duck

Maybe you know this exquisite waterfowl by such names as summer duck, bride, *canard du bois,* plumber, squealer, swamp duck, or wood widgeon, because all of these are common names in scattered parts of America. Even the scientific name of this bird—*Aix sponsa*—translates into wedding dress, which neatly describes the beautiful plumage of the male wood duck.

The wood duck is not really a puddle species and probably doesn't belong in this chapter. However, we will describe it here for convenience and because in many respects it does resemble the teal and its habits are often similar.

The male woody is a striking character no matter whether you find him on the water,

Drake wood duck, a critter which most wildfowlers agree is one of the most exquisite birds on earth. It's a great flyer, too, and delicious on the table. (PHOTO KARL H. MASLOWSKI)

perched in a tree, or flying swiftly past. The easiest characteristics to identify are the white-striped crested head, the white throat, and the dark chest and body. Both drake and hen sit proudly on the water, floating lightly with head and tail erect as if very much on the alert. The most noticeable characteristic of the female is a white ring around the eye and the white throat patch. Otherwise the female appears to be a drab gray bird. The flight of the woody is swift, strong and direct to its target. Because of the white underparts, an observer who doesn't have a very good look at the bird may easily confuse it with a baldpate.

Not too many years ago the population of wood ducks across America reached a low point. Perhaps this can be blamed on the woody's trait of nesting in cavities of hollow trees. As more forests and wood lots were cleared, the number of hollow cavities diminished and so did the

Hen wood duck in springtime. Hen is in typical hollow of tree used for nesting.

number of nesting birds. In recent years, however, waterfowl biologists have devised all sorts of artificial nest boxes, and have succeeded in restoring some of the earlier loss in the population of these birds.

The typical routine of the woody is to rest during the night in open ponds or pools, preferably those located in the middle of woodlands. Then in the early morning it flys out to feeding grounds, in wild-rice marshes, in swamps, along the banks or shores of streams, or in other ponds.

The swift flight of a woody can be all the more exciting because the bird *does* frequent wooded streams and ponds. It can fly through the thickest timber with speed and ease, darting quickly to avoid tree limbs and vegetation, seeming to navigate through impassable places as if with radar and sonar.

On many occasions I have watched from the bank of a woodland pond as at dusk flock after flock of wood ducks came dodging and darting through the trees to finally splash into the water almost at my feet. Several times this gathering of the flocks continued until it was completely dark. Among a thousand memorable waterfowling experiences, these are among the most outstanding.

Found in almost all flyways, but most numerous in the Mississippi flyway, the woody is a rather noisy bird. It is especially noisy when feeding in the woods, where it squeals, clucks, whistles or squeaks continually. Probably the sound most familiar to sportsmen is the *whoo-eek, whoo-eek* which the bird utters when it suddenly senses danger, as when passing close to a duck blind or when spotting a hunter from overhead.

The woody is a grand table bird. I have never eaten very many of them, but those we have prepared for the table would have to be rated second only to the bluewing and greenwing teal.

Ruddy Duck

The ruddy duck or butterball is not a puddle duck. But since it normally dwells in a pond or puddle environment, it will be considered in this chapter for convenience.

The ruddy is a handsome and interesting bird, but not an especially great game bird. It flys well once it completes the laborious chore of get-

ting aloft, although normally it prefers not to fly at all. Curious and somewhat comical in appearance, it is exclusively a North American species. The only other duck to which it is closely related on this continent is the masked duck of Central America.

The number of nicknames used for the ruddy is longer than those for any other duck. A few of the more interesting local names would include booby, booby coot, bristletail, broadbill dipper, bullneck, bumblebee coot, butter duck, dicky duck, dipper duck, dumb bird, dumpling duck, dummy duck, God damn, goose widgeon, hardhead, hickory head, leatherback, little soldier, mud dipper, muskrat duck, paddywack, quilltail coot, rudder bird, rudder duck, shot pouch, shanty duck, sleeping booby, sleepy coot, sleepy jay, soldier duck, spatter duck, spiketail, spoonbill, stifftail, stiffie, toughhead, water partridge, widgeon coot, and wiretail.

No matter whether in bright summer plumage or in dark winter dress, the male ruddy can be quickly identified by its erect fan-shaped tail and its pure-white cheeks overset by a dark skullcap. The animal is also distinctive by being of very short and stubby build.

After rising from the water with great difficulty and after pattering along the surface for a long distance before clearing, the bird has a jerky uneven flight. It appears to be tail-heavy and there is considerable beating of wings during take-off. Both male and female are usually completely silent during flight.

Ruddies nest in central Canada and the U.S. plains states. They winter along our warmer coasts and into Mexico. Autumn migration begins in September and usually follows the main courses of the streams and lakes. Most literature states that the birds fly low and in large flocks. However, in many years and on a number of flyways, I have never seen any very large concentration of ruddy ducks. Probably the longest laps of the flights are made early in the morning or after dusk in the evening.

Even though, as we pointed out, it is not an outstanding game bird, the drake ruddy duck can point to a number of unique distinctions. It has two distinct plumages, one for summer and one for winter. It has the most spectacular of all waterfowl courtship displays. It is the only species to sometimes raise two broods of young in

one season. Except for certain eiders and scoters which are much larger, it lays the largest ducks' eggs. It is also the only duck which possesses an inflatable air sac in the neck, the only duck which carries its tail erect and the only duck which has a really bright blue mandible. However, it is also among the most helpless of all ducks on land. It has been pointed out that although it is very rare for any female duck to be silent, the female ruddy is.

Other ducks that American gunners might conceivably encounter, especially if they hunt along our southern border and in Mexico, are the masked duck, the black-bellied tree duck and the fulvous tree duck. But none of these birds frequently ventures north of the border, and so they are not especially important in this discussion. Nor do they belong rightfully to the classification of puddle duck. Still another puddle duck, the European teal, which closely resembles our greenwing teal, may be encountered by northern gunners. This also is so rare as not to be considered important here.

Author holds up brace of baldpates bagged on shallow marsh at west end of Lake Erie.

Chapter 3

DIVING DUCKS

More often than not our diving ducks frequent the larger, deeper lakes and rivers plus our coastal areas, lagoons and inlets. This is not a hard-and-fast rule, but normally they feed more by diving than do puddle ducks, and they can feed this way at considerable depths. To escape danger they can travel great distances under water, emerging only enough to show their heads or bill tips before submerging again.

Altogether about forty-three forms of diving ducks exist on the earth and twenty of these are found at one time or another in North America.

The diving ducks lack the brilliance of the speculum of the puddle ducks. But still there are important field marks in most species. Since most have small tails, their huge paddle feet may be used as rudders in flight and are often visible to good observers of the flying birds. When launch-

Scene on a rocky Lake Erie reef. Although decoys here are for puddle ducks and/or nondescript, buffleheads and scaup found it attractive.

ing into flight, most of this group patter along the water before becoming airborne.

The diets of diving ducks consist to a greater extent of shellfish, mollusks and aquatic plants, which make them a second choice generally to sportsmen. But canvasbacks and redheads fattened on eel grass or wild celery are notable exceptions. Although not highly esteemed by every gunner, even bluebills are often very delicious to eat.

Since the wings of diving ducks are small in proportion to the size and weight of their bodies, they have a very rapid wingbeat when compared to puddle ducks. This is one method of waterfowl identification which is commonly used throughout the country.

Canvasbacks

To many the canvasback is the greatest game bird in the world, both because of its speed on the wing and because of its high reputation among epicures. It surely deserves recognition on both counts. Canvasbacks are among our easiest birds to identify. First, they are quite large. Second, even at a considerable distance the long bill and elongated head are noticeable and will distinguish them from redheads, with which they often join company. However, the best means of identification is the extreme whiteness of the back of the male duck. The female, although darker than the drake, has the same general outline of head and body. All canvasbacks sit low on the water. When about to dive, the species throws itself upward and forward as if to launch itself into the descent.

In flight the main recognition marks of the canvasback are its large size, white body and long slender dark-headed neck. The wings are long and pointed but of small surface compared to the heavy body. It is miraculous that wings of this size can give such terrific speed and suggest such great power in flight. Canvasbacks migrate in formations which constantly shift between wavy lines and regular V's. Smaller flocks occasionally fly in irregular compact formation.

The main breeding grounds of canvasbacks are on the western Canadian prairie extending far to the north. There is also a small island of breeding area in Alaska. Canvasbacks winter all along our Pacific coast and down through the western half of Mexico. They also winter along our Atlantic coast from New York southward to Louisiana, and along the Gulf coast of Mexico. Ordinarily the bird is a late migrant, and it often stays in the north until freezing ponds, heavy snowstorms and extremely cold weather drive it southward.

Canvasback shooting is good any time but probably never better than during a bad storm, when the birds move downwind at incredible speeds. The most famous wintering area for canvasbacks is the region along the coast of Virginia and North Carolina. They gather there in vast numbers in the company of other diving ducks to feed on the roots, seeds, grass and other vegetation which is especially to their liking.

The delicate and delicious flavor of canvasback ducks has been discussed so often elsewhere, in fact wherever waterfowlers gather, that it is also worth discussing here. It is true that the average canvasback must rate with the most delicious of all ducks. It could be attributed to the species' liking of wild celery buds and the fact that wild celery in some areas furnishes a great part of the canvasback's diet. This isn't necessarily true, however, because on the Pacific coast where wild celery is not found, canvasbacks rely to a great extent upon a plant called wapatoo, and there the flesh is just as delicious as is the celery-feeding birds of the eastern seaboard.

Several years ago while hunting for blacks and mallards along the Ohio River near New Richmond, Ohio, canvasbacks kept coming in to our decoys until we had collected two full limits of them. As a result we made great preparations for a game dinner later on. But if all ducks turned out to be as unpleasant to eat as these, the number of duck hunters would be greatly curtailed. These cans had a strong and fishy taste. And this is not an isolated situation, because on the Pacific coast, canvasbacks have occasionally been known to feed or even to gorge on the rotting flesh of spawned-out salmon, and when they do so they are not fit to eat.

Sometimes the canvasback is a most wary bird and very difficult to approach. But in early autumn the young birds and the new arrivals southward usually decoy very easily. Once they have encountered shooting and shooters, they rapidly become more shy and eventually must be considered among the most clever of all our native waterfowl.

Redheads

The American redhead or the American pochard ranges from the Atlantic to the Pacific coasts and is as often as not found with the canvasback, which it somewhat resembles. But the closer the inspection the less it is found to resemble the canvasback. Only the red-brown head of the male and the neutral color of the body of the female are similar. The male redhead has a puffy-round dark head and chest and a grayish body, whereas the canvasback's body shows up as almost pure white.

Redheads have more tendency than most other ducks to gather in very large rafts and to spend the days in deep open water. Only bad storms break up these rafts into smaller groups and drive them into smaller water areas. They do fly out regularly in morning and evening to feed in shallower places.

The redhead does not breed and nest as far north as the canvasback, since its main nesting area lies in central Canada and the north-central United States. This fact no doubt has contributed much to its alarming decrease in recent years. Too much of the land normally in the redhead's breeding range has been drained and otherwise used for agricultural purposes. It has often been stated that the decrease in redhead numbers can be attributed to shooting by sportsmen and to the annual open seasons on the bird. However, the nesting range is a vastly more important factor. Even a series of closed seasons on the

Drake redhead, a member of the pochard family, is one of the world's greatest game birds. (PHOTO KARL H. MASLOWSKI)

bird, during which no shooting of the bird was permitted, did not greatly increase its numbers in recent years.

Wintering areas for the redhead are widely separated. One concentration is located along the coast of Virginia and North Carolina. The other wintering area includes the coast of California, the Texas and Louisiana Gulf coast plus the northern half of Mexico. These handsome ducks migrate between summer and winter area in V-shaped fairly regular flocks. But during movements from resting to feeding grounds during the day, they move in much larger flocks and in an irregular formation. This is the way hunters will ordinarily see them.

While flying, redheads appear shorter and darker than canvasbacks. The wings seem to beat more rapidly and the flight seems to be more erratic. They also seem to arise from the water in a confused manner and always appear to be in a hurry. Often when rafting or resting in open water the flock will suddenly boil up for no apparent reason and then just as quickly settle down again.

Male redheads make very little sound except an occasional soft purring which resembles that of a tomcat. Occasionally in autumn, males may also give a weak quack-quack. Females are much noisier and when flushed from the water they make a loud clear quack which is higher in tone than the quack of a mallard or black duck.

The main autumn migration from nesting to wintering area is well under way during October. Sometimes they travel in company with canvasbacks on these migrations and sometimes with scaup, and on still other occasions they have been observed traveling alone. Occasionally migrating flocks will pause in the Great Lakes area and linger there all winter long if ice does not cover the entire lake surface. The redhead is just as good and can be just as bad on the table as a canvasback. No doubt this is a matter of the bird's diet.

Greater Scaup

Among the game birds most frequently underrated by North American sportsmen is the greater scaup. It is a handsome sturdy bird which superficially resembles the redhead and which is a strong fast flyer. Probably its name is derived from its habit of feeding around oyster and mussel beds, which in Europe and Scotland are called scaup beds. It may also have been named for its characteristic cry of *scaup-scaup*.

In much of the United States the greater scaup is known as the bluebill or lake bluebill. But by any name it is very similar to the lesser scaup and it is very difficult to distinguish between the two in the field. The greater scaup weighs slightly more than the lesser scaup. Also the gloss of the nearly black head of the greater scaup tends to be green as compared to the purple gloss in a lesser scaup.

Virtually the entire breeding range of the greater scaup is confined to Alaska and the Yukon territory. Two separate wintering areas exist, one along our northern Pacific coast and the other along the Atlantic coast from New England southward to North Carolina. A number of birds also winter in the eastern Great Lakes region. On the wintering grounds, greater scaup prefer the larger bodies of water, where they ordinarily gather in huge rafts during the daytime. Rough or choppy water doesn't seem to bother them; in fact, they seem to enjoy it.

Scaup travel from place to place in rather compact formations, and the speed of their flight

Greater scaup drake. (PHOTO KARL H. MASLOW-SKI)

is rapid. The wings produce a loud rustling sound and if it is a very large flock this sound is almost a roar. During longer migrations they have been observed by pilots at very high altitudes. But when traveling between feeding areas, they normally fly very low. A good way to distinguish the greater scaup from the lesser scaup in flight is the longer light strip which shows through the wing.

Of all ducks, the greater scaup is one of the most difficult to kill. Gunners who are not good marksmen or who shoot at these birds at long range lose far too many of them. Unless a scaup is mortally hit on the first shot it will dive repeatedly and never come up again until it is far away from the shooter. They are also better able to elude retrievers than most other ducks, which cannot dive so well.

Another common characteristic of the greater scaup is as follows: When resting on the sea or a large lake, they often sit in an unbroken line parallel to the coast or shore. Suddenly a bird at one end of the line will take wing, and it will then be followed in order right along the line to the last bird. To see this maneuver in the distance is to be almost certain that you have seen a flock of greater scaup.

Greater scaup are late migrants and they seem to thrive on the storms and high winds which appear to accompany them toward their wintering grounds. Some of the best shooting I can recall occurred on mornings when the bluebills were flying and decoying into winds of nearly hurricane proportions. The birds would swarm downwind, turn suddenly, bank, and slip almost without motion in to the decoys.

Lesser Scaup

Lesser scaup or little bluebills are lively and restless ducks no matter whether on the water or in the air. They often swim about or flush for no apparent reason. They migrate very late and often move south just ahead of freeze-up. On local flights they travel in closely bunched flocks that move and dart erratically, twisting and turning often. On long migration flights they stay fairly high.

This handsome species is exclusively a North American duck and it is widely distributed across the continent. It tends more to inland lakes, ponds and marshes than other divers, although it does winter along all of our seacoasts. Many bluebills go beyond the continental

Lesser scaup, two males and female. (PHOTO KARL H. MASLOWSKI)

United States to winter in Mexico, Cuba, Puerto Rico, and other points south.

The normal nesting range of lesser scaup includes most of the Dakotas and western and northwestern Canada, extending somewhat into Alaska. Next to the whitewing scoters, they are the latest breeders of all continental waterfowl. Their broods do not hatch until early in July, and since ten or eleven weeks are necessary before the young are able to fly, the autumn migration is necessarily very late. The birds are equally as late in returning to the nesting areas in the springtime, a fact which explains why so many of them are seen in late spring throughout the central United States.

Bluebills are not held in the highest regard as food by most sportsmen. But birds taken at inland points early in the season invariably are tender and do not have the fishy taste which is generally associated with them.

This much is certain: the lesser scaup is a fast-flying, exciting target on every flyway. Since it is a relatively abundant duck, it furnishes tremendous sport for American gunners. It is also a duck whose numbers have not declined so alarmingly as some other species in recent years.

Ringneck Duck

The ringneck duck, which has a ring around its bill rather than around its neck, is another species which has many local names and curious nicknames. Among these are: blackhead, black-

Handsome drake ringneck duck. Color and shape of head make this one fairly easy to identify.

jack, buckeye, foul duck, moonbill, mud duck, ringbill, ringbill shuffler and priest duck. By any name it is a handsome bird and one which is fairly easy to identify both in flight and on the water.

The male appears as a very black duck but with gray flanks that seem almost white. A white crescent at the lower part of the wing is noticeable at very long distances. Perhaps it is because the rest of the duck is so dark, but at closer ranges the white rings on the bill can also be easily noticed.

In the air, ringnecks travel in rather small flocks usually of less than a dozen birds in an open formation, and they go swiftly and directly toward their target. They usually alight without circling and in this manner surprise many hunters by dropping so suddenly in to the decoys. On the wing they can be mistaken for scaups and redheads. The females are easily confused with the females of other diving species.

More than any other divers, ringnecks are essentially a fresh-water species, being most abundant in the interior of the United States. They greatly prefer sloughs, marshes and lagoons to open lakes. Like scaup, however, they are very nervous and alert birds. Extremely good divers, they can obtain food in water as deep as forty feet and have been captured by accident in the nets of fishermen at this depth. Although they must run along the surface of the water in the manner of all divers during take-off, the actual take-off is accomplished with much greater ease than with the other diving ducks. Ringnecks make an unmistakable whistle of the wings as they flush and as they fly past a blind.

The main nesting area of ringnecks extends from northern Minnesota and the upper Great Lakes region into south-central Canada. The greatest migration begins during the middle of October, before the scaup's, and ends in November. By that time most nesting birds have passed southward over the Canadian border and are well on their way toward wintering areas.

The ringneck's main wintering area is confined to the southeast quarter of the United States. Another smaller area is located in northern California and Oregon.

Ringnecks are not especially shy or intelligent ducks when compared to their cousins. They have an unfortunate habit of returning again and again to a certain pond, even after having encountered shooters there on earlier trips. On the table the ringneck must rank with the finest of all ducks. The meat is mild, delicious and tender, and most ringnecks are extremely fat when taken in the early fall. Ringneck hens are largely silent and males make a soft purring noise.

American Goldeneye

Here is another species of waterfowl which has many local names. Among these are brasseye, whistler, bright-eye, copperhead, fiddler duck, ice duck, ironhead, little diver, oyster duck, pie duck, pied whistler, sleepy diver, whistle diver, whistle duck and winter duck.

Toward the tag end of the waterfowl season in many areas, the goldeneye furnishes all the shooting that is left after other birds have passed on southward to warmer places. It isn't a game bird in the same class as the other divers, but on the wing it is a fast and often elusive target.

Goldeneyes are wary birds, and while they will come in to decoys, they have a habit of shying off and away just before they are in range. On other maddening occasions they will fly in toward the decoys and then alight on the water beyond the decoys, also out of range. Then other birds will join them.

Small dark-headed ducks with white patches on the cheeks, the American goldeneye breeds and nests completely across Canada from Newfoundland to the Bering Sea. Their winter range is everywhere in the United States except the southwest and the extreme southeast. They do not mind extremely cold weather and any lake which is not completely frozen over is a potential winter resting site for these handsome little birds.

The common nickname of whistler comes from the distinctive whistling sound of wings when the bird is in flight. Ordinarily they move in small flocks often high in the air. When they rise from the water, they rise in rapid spirals. They are ordinarily considered as exceedingly wary, but on float trips for jump-shooting ducks on Ohio rivers, it has been easy to drift within a few feet of goldeneyes.

Although both male and female are usually quiet birds, drakes can utter a piercing, *spear-*

Drake Barrow's goldeneye, a rarely photographed bird. (PHOTO BY KARL H. MASLOWSKI)

spear sound. Hens have only a low quack. American goldeneyes are not especially good on the table. I have cooked them in a number of different ways but no method I have tried is really successful.

A close cousin of the American goldeneye exists only west of the Rocky Mountains. It is the Barrow's goldeneye and differs only in that it has a white crescent in front of the eye of the male. It isn't very abundant and is not a very important duck from the standpoint of duck hunting.

Bufflehead

Here is another species peculiar to North America. Originally it was called buffalo head (and buffalo duck) because of the unusual shape of its head, but this has been reduced to bufflehead and elsewhere the duck is known as butterball. Only slightly larger than teal, bufflehead are among the world's smallest ducks. The male appears as largely white with an enormous black head marked with a triangular white crest. It can be confused with a male hooded mer-

Labrador retrieves male bufflehead.

ganser but the silhouette of the two birds is entirely different. The bufflehead is short and
stubby.

Many sportsmen will not be bothered with
hunting buffleheads, but shooters during late
season around the Lake Erie islands have found
that this bird has many sporting qualities. It flys
low to the water, is fast and has rapid wingbeats.
It travels in small flocks and can flush straight
upward to become airborne. A very late season
migrant, it will remain as far north as open
water permits. Ordinarily silent, drake buffle-

heads may give a squeaking call, and they also
have a low guttural note. Hens quack very
weakly.

Old Squaw

This unique but handsome bird is known only
to a few shooters along the upper Atlantic coast,
in the Puget Sound area and in the Great Lakes
region. Although it is the most expert diver
among native ducks, it is not very good to eat
and is not an especially good game bird. It is

Hunter crouched on Lake Erie island for pass shooting at buffleheads, some bald-pates.

The northern eider is an arctic species which hunters in the United States never see.

worth noting, however, that they have been found in commercial fishing nets as deep as one hundred feet in the Great Lakes. There is one report of over fifteen hundred old squaws being caught through a haul of a gill net in the Great Lakes area. The male old squaw can be identified instantly at any time of the year by its characteristic long tail. In winter the male plumage is generally piebald and mostly white with white head and neck. In summer it is mostly brown with brown head and neck. The male sits very low on the water with his head erect and his tail well elevated, except when feeding. It isn't possible to confuse this duck with a pintail, which also has a long tail, because the old squaw is much more chunky of build.

An extremely garrulous and noisy bird, old squaws decoy very well. They seem to be tame, trusting and full of curiosity. This makes them on the whole very easy targets. However, some old squaws seem almost immune to shot, and unless the bird is killed outright it is difficult to retrieve. To pursue a slightly wounded bird is almost useless because of its incredible diving ability.

A number of other ducks can well be included in the category of diving ducks, but none of these are vigorously pursued by sportsmen. Nor are any of them especially good on the table. Included in this category would be the common merganser, the red-breasted merganser, the hooded merganser, the surf scoter, common scoter and whitewing scoter, and the eider ducks.

Chapter 4

GEESE AND BRANT

A sportsman might spend a good portion of his life wandering around the world as I have and never quite match the thrill of a misty morning in a Kentucky cornfield. The day was cold, unpleasantly cold. The earth into which my pit blind had been excavated was frozen granite hard. A gray fog, maybe it was a shroud of frost crystals, hovered over the bottom. I could scarcely see the man in the next pit light his cigarette only fifty feet away.

As we waited, I wondered about something I had pondered over before. Why does a man go goose hunting? But in the next instant I knew. The honking was faint and far away at first, but it raised goose pimples just as it had when the phrase was coined a long time ago. As the honking came closer it became a haunting klaxon call which added a chill that played up and down my spine. No sound, it seems to me, unless it would be the hunting cry of a timber-wolf pack, is more primitive or more symbolic of the lonely places left in North America.

The geese came closer, and although I couldn't see them, I did hear the beating of powerful wings overhead. This circling and descending can shake even the veteran hunter who is rock steady on a deer stand. Then all at once the geese were down on top of me and my decoys. Who can describe what really happens at a moment like this?

When it was all over and the sound of honking faded, I had a fine fat gander for two easy shots. Did I say easy? I also had a pounding heart, a case of buck fever that wouldn't go away, and an indelible memory.

"This," I said to the man who had lit the ciga-rette and who had also bagged a goose, "should happen to every American who owns a fowling piece."

And maybe it will.

The truth is that few of our outdoor sports to-day have such a promising future as goose hunting. There was a time when only a few lucky sportsmen could have a whirl at it and a wild honker was a relatively rare trophy. But happily that picture is changing. Now anyone can enjoy a wild-goose chase and no pun is intended.

Consider these important points. Although ducks seem on the decline and shooting them is becoming more and more restricted, our goose population is holding its own. It may even be increasing slightly. Here is a bird our wildlife biologists have found which can actually be managed and encouraged. And although its normal nesting range is so remote and sometimes in such inhospitable climate that it has discouraged agriculture and drainage, the goose can be induced to nest elsewhere, as we will see.

Of all the North American geese, sportsmen are concerned mostly with three: the Canada, the blue and the snow. They are by far the most abundant. However, hunters may also occasionally encounter the white-fronted goose, the emperor goose and Ross's goose.

Canada Goose

The designation Canada goose covers several closely related cousins that vary mostly in size, from the three-and-a-half-pound-average Rich-

Goose hunting near Eagle Lake, Texas, in rice fields for blues, snows, and white-fronts. Notice white suits of hunters—and white cards used for decoys.

ardson's goose through the cackling goose, the lesser Canada and the common Canada, which averages eight or nine pounds. All look pretty much the same, with black necks and white cheeks. There isn't much value in exploring other differences, because ornithologists themselves do not always agree on the classification of these birds.

The common Canada goose or honker or Canadian honker is surely one of the most magnificent birds in the world. Whether resting on water or grazing on land, these brownish-gray geese with long black necks held straight up-

Flock of Canada geese suddenly alerted—photo made near Moiese, Montana.

right are easy to recognize. The white cheek patches and the clearly defined base of the black stocking are characteristic and easy to notice. Honkers swim gracefully in the manner of swans and they can swim rapidly if necessary. Considering their size and structure, they are also very agile on land.

During flight, the large gray bodies and long black necks of Canada geese are also unmistakable. On short flights they may travel in small compact flights and give the impression that their flying is labored or very difficult. But during high-altitude or migration travel, their flight seems extremely graceful. During these migrations the geese fly in the familiar undulating V-shaped formations which sometimes change to a long single line or Indian file. Rising from land or water, geese ordinarily take several steps to gain take-off. When suddenly surprised, they can spring into the air with a single bound.

The wariness and intelligence of Canadian honkers is as well known as their characteristic honking cry. Whenever feeding, either on land or water, it always seems that at least part of the flock are on the alert for approaching danger. A warning from any one of the birds, and

Greatest sight in goose hunter's world is when Canadas set their wings, as here, to descend toward decoys.

all necks suddenly raise and in the next instant the flock is airborne. They evidently have very keen eyesight and their hearing is remarkable.

The various kinds of Canadas nest almost completely across Canada and in portions of the northwestern United States and into Alaska. In several states in the eastern half of the United States, local goose flocks have been established or are in the process of being established. The basis or core of such a process is a large lake or marsh that becomes a refuge. Here a flock of geese can rest or loiter and never be disturbed.

The Canada-goose flock is established in var-ious ways, at first by feeding or baiting heavily to arrest wild birds during mid-migration and later by encouraging them to nest, thereby building a native flock. These wild geese tend to nest in the places where they learn to fly, and an increasing number of birds return to the local refuges each fall. This scheme, which has great promise, will supplement the production of geese in the far north with non-migratory birds reared at points throughout the country.

In Missouri in 1963 during a sixty-day goose season, 14,600 birds were bagged around the Swan Lake National Wild Life Refuge and the

Hunter in central Ohio cornfield. Decoys are papier-mâché and the blind is a shallow pit covered with cornstalks.

adjacent Fountain Grove State Wildlife area. In addition, 3000 honkers were taken in the vicinity of the Squaw Creek Wildlife Refuge.

Other Canada-goose flocks have been established in Minnesota at Red Lake, Agassiz and Tamarack National Wildlife Refuges; in Illinois, at Horseshoe Lake, Union County and Crab Orchard; in Nebraska at Crescent Lake; in North Dakota at Upper and Lower Souris; in South Dakota at Lacreek, Sand Lake and Waubay; in Wisconsin at Necedah and Horicon Marsh; in Michigan at Seney and Shiawassee National Wildlife Refuges, Allegan County; in Tennes-

see at Chickamauga Lake; in South Carolina at the Santee Cooper System; in Maryland in Kent County; in Ontario at Jack Miner Sanctuary; in Kentucky in Ballard County; in Ohio at Lake Saint Marys, Mosquito Reservoir, Mercer County, O'Shaughnessy Reservoir; in Pennsylvania at Pymatuning Reservoir; in Indiana at Hovey Lake.

Of course, there are many other goose concentrations besides these, especially in the west, where it hasn't been necessary to build captive or artificial flocks. A list of these places would be almost impossible to compile, but a good ex-

Typical goose blind in the east—in this case at Lake Mattamuskeet, N.C. (STATE OF NORTH CAROLINA PHOTO BY BILL GULLEY)

Goose hunter at Lake Mattamuskeet, N.C. The tower is a famous landmark for waterfowlers hereabouts. (NORTH CAROLINA WILDLIFE RESOURCES COMMISSION PHOTO BY JACK DERMID)

ample is the Missouri River bottom-land area south of Helena, Montana. Another is the Arkansas River bottoms of Colorado.

A hunter's best bet is to contact his state conservation department for information on these goose areas. In some cases the hunt as well as the flocks are controlled. Hunting is permitted on an allotment or lottery basis and sometimes there is a nominal fee for blinds and transportation to them.

Blue Goose

In many ways the handsome blue goose is a very mysterious bird. For many years it wasn't even known where the bird nested. Now it has been established that the main nesting area is the tundra region of Baffin Island and adjacent land areas in extreme northern Canada. Since blue geese and snow geese are known to interbreed very readily, there is also considerable disagreement among ornithologists and biologists about whether blues or snows are separate species of birds or whether they are color variations of one and the same goose.

But no matter what his origin or classification, the blue goose is a fine game bird averaging about five pounds when fully grown. It is a medium-size goose with gray-and-brown underparts and a white head and neck. Its bill is pink.

Both on the water and in flight it is best distinguished by the all-white neck and head. It can be confused only with the emperor goose, which is different in that it is black on the underside of its neck.

During flight, blue geese fly in an uneven or broken mixture of V's and irregular lines. During migration they are often found with snow geese and occasionally even with some of the smaller Canadas. When flying they constantly call with a high pitched *goop, goop*, which can easily be distinguished from the honking of Canada geese.

In late August and early September blues and snows in the far northern nesting grounds become restless and gather in larger and larger flocks, which then begin the long migration southward. This migration follows the shore of Hudson Bay and James Bay, where nearly all

Blue goose in Texas. (U. S. FISH AND WILDLIFE SERVICE PHOTO BY N. KENT)

the blue geese on the continent seem to gather in early fall.

Outfitters annually fly hundreds of sportsmen up to the James Bay region for the spectacular shooting. There Cree guides put out goose-wing decoys on the golden arctic grasslands and call these big birds to gunpoint. When not hunting, the sportsmen live in comfortable quarters provided by the outfitter. These packaged trips are moderately expensive; figure on $300 to $400 a week. But it is a grand opportunity to see remote and lonely country and at the same time to become better acquainted with a splendid North American game bird.

Snow Goose

Two kinds of snow geese, greater and lesser, are native to North America. Both nest in the extreme Canadian north and both are favorites with American sportsmen. Completely snow white of plumage except for black wing tips, the snow goose is called ghost goose by the Cree Indians and elsewhere is known as wa-wa, the Indian name for wild goose. In our southern states it is commonly called a white brant.

By way of comparing the different snow geese, the greater snow geese average six or

Snow geese. (PHOTO BY KARL H. MASLOWSKI)

It is interesting to note that the nesting area of Ross's goose was not discovered until 1940 by Charles Gillham, a U. S. Fish and Wildlife Service biologist.

Snow geese are never hard to identify except from one another. Only our swans are all white in plumage, but there can be no confusion here in identification. Swans fly high with slower wingbeats and their necks are much longer than the short neck of the snow goose. Except perhaps for very young birds very early in the season, snow geese are shy and wary. They fly high and fast in long diagonal lines or in V flocks, usually calling shrilly as they go. When a flock of white geese pass silently overhead, it is safe to assume that they are Ross's geese because these are silent during flight.

Emperor Goose

This is the least known of all American geese, probably because it never leaves Alaska. Known widely among Alaskans as the Eskimo or painted goose, it nests in the coastal areas along the Bering Sea and its migration to wintering areas is only a short hop to points along the Alaskan peninsula and the Aleutian Islands. The emperor is a medium-size handsome bird. On the water in good sunlight its body may appear a silvery gray. It resembles the blue goose except for the black marking on the underside of the neck. This same black neck marking is its best identification during flight.

The voice of the emperor goose is more shrill and differs from that of any other goose. During flight it constantly calls a shrill *klaha, klaha, klaha,* and when feeding it uses a great variety of conversational grunts and other sounds.

Emperor geese average about six or six and a half pounds in weight. There is great disagreement as to their quality as table birds, although Eskimos along the western Alaskan coast depend upon them for food and for feathers.

American Brant

The American brant is a handsome small goose not much larger than a mallard or a canvasback duck. It is truly a sea goose, since it is seldom found very far away from salt water. It is an extremely graceful, swift-flying bird. On

Lesser snow goose at Texas wintering area. (U. S. FISH AND WILDLIFE SERVICE PHOTO BY W. F. KUBICHEK)

Ross's goose, a fairly rare bird.

seven pounds in weight; the lesser snow goose averages about five pounds in weight. Ross's goose, which appears to be a miniature snow goose, averages about two and a half pounds. Lesser snow geese winter along the Louisiana and Texas Gulf coast and in central California. Greater snow geese winter along the Atlantic coast from Virginia southward to North Carolina. Ross's goose, which is not especially abundant, concentrates its wintering in central California.

the water it sits as high and lightly as a gull, with tail up-raised and its head poised. In the air it can flash downwind past a blind before a hunter has time to flip the safety of his gun.

American brant nest as far north in Canada as any other game birds. There is also a nesting colony along the northwest shore of Greenland. All of their wintering is confined to the Atlantic coast from Connecticut to North Carolina, an area where a chief food, eel grass, grows extensively in shallow bays and estuaries. Unlike geese, these brant do not often feed on land but rather follow the ebbing tide to find the food they need. They do not often dive for food but feed by tipping as do the puddle ducks.

Most sportsmen who know them agree that the American brant is one of the finest game birds of all on the table. The meat is consistently tender, delicate and mild in flavor. In the old days of market hunting, brant often commanded the highest prices of any waterfowl.

On the water the brant appears as a very dark, almost black, goose with whitish or gray sides. These same characteristics are evident when in flight. It can be most easily confused with its first cousin, the black brant of the Pacific, but its sides do not show as much white as the Pacific bird. American brant fly in long, wavy, undulating lines and sometimes in regular V-formations. Their voices, which are loud and metallic, can often be heard a long distance away.

Three photos made hunting snows and blues near Fort Albany on the west shore of James Bay, Ontario. Perhaps this is the greatest goose shooting in America.

Black Brant

The black brant, which is very similar in appearance and habits to the American brant, is confined to the Pacific coast. It nests along the north shore of Alaska and eastward toward the Mackenzie Delta of Canada. It winters along our Pacific coast from Puget Sound southward through Baja California. In the latter place I have found it abundant along sand beaches, where fast evening shooting is possible as late as March.

As pointed out before, it is very difficult to distinguish the black brant from the American brant, but there is no point in explaining the differences in detail. The birds simply are never seen together. The flight of the black brant is fast, as the bird moves with rapid wing strokes and often travels very close to the water. It frequently changes elevation, probably moving up and down with existing wind currents. During flight it offers a low guttural sound that almost resembles a growling. Like the American brant, it is delicious on the table.

Perhaps the most delicious single waterfowl meal I can remember occurred the golden evening Glenn Lau and I sat in camp beside a lonely Baja California lagoon in the rapidly falling night. Tired from a long day of driving over a rocky road and primed with tequila, we broiled the fillets of several brant over an open fire

while basting them with lime juice and olive oil. No duck—in fact, no game at all—ever tasted any better.

White-Fronted Goose

The white-fronted or speckled-belly goose is a bird that only western gunners are likely to see. It nests in northern Alaska and extreme northwestern Canada and then winters along the Texas and Louisiana Gulf coast, in northwestern Mexico and in central California. It is a very handsome and striking bird, very good on the table, but probably the least sophisticated of all our native geese. On a number of occasions I have seen this species fly within easy range of gunners who were standing unconcealed and in the open. Often it travels in the company of blue and snow geese.

This bird can be identified on the water because it is the only goose with brown head, chest, neck and underparts. The white front for which it is named isn't too visible except during flight. If not too far away, the barred black-and-white breast is also a good mark of identification during flight. During migration they fly high in V-shaped flocks and therefore somewhat resemble Canada geese. Their call uttered in flight is a cackle, which some gunners have described as laughter.

As we have pointed out, all of the North American geese are migrants. They nest and summer in the north mostly in Canada and winter in the United States. But under normal conditions they also make daily migrations; two round trips, morning and evening, from nesting grounds or refuge areas to feeding areas. The feeding areas may be on land or water, but most likely are on land because geese are grazers. Hunting them is generally planned to take advantage of these daily migrations.

There are a number of ways to hunt geese. For instance, when they are loitering along the river it is possible to camouflage a canoe or shallow-draft skiff to resemble a pile of debris and to drift downstream in to shooting range. This method is described as duck freelancing in another chapter, but for geese it is a pretty chancy method. So is stalking them on foot.

Geese on the ground, except in long-established refuges, are extremely wary. Stalking them successfully is usually a slow and tedious process during which a sportsman must take every advantage of cover and terrain. But usually there is little cover and nine times in ten the stalker must crawl face down on either a frozen turf or through gumbo mud.

Flyway shooting is by far the deadliest technique. First you locate your flock of geese, then observe its flight route between nesting and feeding areas. It is along this route that a man finds his shooting.

But how do you find resting and feeding grounds? Sometimes with field glasses. Other times you may have to follow the flying birds, at a distance naturally, in a car across the countryside. It's a good idea to ask farmers and rural mail carriers to keep you posted on feeding flights.

When you have located a feeding area, you are ready to go hunting. If the geese have not been molested on an evening flight, they will

A Cree Indian housewife plucks geese for James Bay hunters.

probably follow the same route the next morning, and vice versa. Your next step is to find a good interception point somewhere along the flight route. You dig a pit or build a blind, put out a spread of decoys, and wait hopefully. But it may be a long uncomfortable wait.

Whereas smaller waterfowl begin to move at daybreak and even before dawn regardless of weather, geese are much more leisurely. If the weather is bad they may not begin to fly until midmorning. A homeward evening flight may start in midafternoon. Occasionally geese may be coming and going at the same time, with the flight continuing all day long. At such times a clever hunter can station himself so as to enjoy a bit of pass shooting.

This flight-interception strategy will work anywhere in America, with regional variations. In Texas, for example, the blues fly to rice fields to feed, in Maryland the Canadas look for cornfields and in the Dakotas you'll find geese in wheat stubble. Differences in blinds and decoys vary geographically too.

Somebody once said geese can be the dumbest and wisest of all birds, and there is evidence to support this comment. For instance, they often show great gullibility about decoys. On a hunt at Eagle Lake, Texas, I was amazed to find that my guide carried several dozen white "Tom Mc-Cready for Sheriff" placards to be used as decoys. He folded each just once and scattered them at random around a pit he had dug.

Maryland hunter with big honkers bagged from a cornfield blind.

"We look more like litterbugs," I commented, "than goose hunters."

"Baby diapers work just as well," he answered, "but after the election these are free."

The placards worked unbelievably well. We bagged six mixed geese, the legal limit at the time, and then settled back to watch the marvelous spectacle of geese winging everywhere on the horizon.

That morning we also witnessed one of the most ludicrous wildlife spectacles I've ever seen. A white-fronted goose dropped out of his flight to land among the cardboards, and he wasn't at all dismayed to find out he had been fooled. He actually poked his head under several posters as if to read them. He hung around so long, in fact, that I had to cough to get rid of him.

Expert goose hunters are divided on the matter of calls, but almost all depend on one to supplement their decoys. Calling, however, is such a vast and complicated subject that it can't be tackled here. The beginner would do well to let a guide or experienced hand do the calling. Or he might visit a refuge and try to imitate what he hears there. Another alternative is to buy one of the call records now available and to begin practicing.

Goose hunting is a great sport any way you look at it, but it is never more exciting than the day you yourself call a goose in to shotgun range.

Sunset on a Canada goose resting area in Maryland.

Chapter 5

MYSTERY BIRDS OF THE MARSHES

It may sound strange to sportsmen elsewhere across the land, but some of America's most traditional hunting depends on a high tide along the Atlantic seaboard and on a bird few hunters know. It begins in September, as it has since colonial times, when tides flood the estuaries, the river mouths and the salt-water flats from New England southward to the Carolinas. It's then and there that clapper rails—the "railbirds" of the Jersey shore and the "marsh hens" of Chesapeake Bay—are most abundant and therefore ready for autumn's harvest.

Classic railbirding has changed very little since the first generation of rail hunters set the pattern. Today, as always, it's a two-man team affair: one man to stand and shoot; another to pole a double-ended boat through the flooded marsh grasses. Even the boat's design is little-altered since those early days. One old reference described a railbirding boat like this: "Square ends front and back, with a draft shallow enough to follow a mule as it sweats up a dusty road." Craft that closely fit these specifications are standard to this day on the Connecticut, the Choptank, the Delaware and on any other river in clapper country. The sport is as popular as ever thereabouts.

Even though rail hunting has persisted along the seaboard, it never really caught on in mid-United States, where other species of rails are actually more plentiful than clappers are along the coast. It seems incredible in these times of limited game-bags that game birds by the mil-lions can funnel down our flyways every autumn and be almost completely ignored by American hunters. But it's true. Seasons on them are long (up to seventy days), bag limits are liberal (up to twenty-five per day in some cases) and there are splendid gunning possibilities in nearly every state. But still, and this is certainly incredible, few sportsmen even know that these mystery birds—gallinules as well as rails—exist.

During the peaks of migrations rails swarm in swamps and marshlands in every state of the Union, but because of their secretive habits and perhaps because of their mysterious arrival American gunners have never become acquainted with them. Result: an astronomical amount of sport is wasted annually. Vast quantities of delicious meat never go into home freezers. And an unnecessary void occurs every year between the fishing and hunting seasons. Too many Indian summers are wasted.

Six kinds of rails (soras, kings, Virginias, clappers and the rarely killed black rails and yellow rails) and two kinds of gallinules (Floridas and purples) comprise this unharvested resource. At least one of these species, usually several, is native in every corner of the land. At least one, but more than likely several, passes through every shallow wetland en route from nesting grounds in the north (often in the far north) to wintering areas in the Caribbean or points still farther south.

The soras, or Carolina rails, are the most abundant of all. They're the most widely distributed

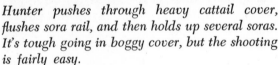

Hunter pushes through heavy cattail cover, flushes sora rail, and then holds up several soras. It's tough going in boggy cover, but the shooting is fairly easy.

because they nest in bogs and marshes everywhere across the northern United States and all through Canada. They're prolific breeders and during a fall migration will suddenly descend on marshy areas in astonishing numbers. Just as suddenly, almost, when the temperature falls or when there is a heavy frost, they disappear again, headed farther south. Nowadays when anyone mentions rail shooting in mid-America, he's probably speaking of soras.

Averaging eight or nine inches long and weighing about half as much as an average bobwhite, soras are brownish in color and have chicken-like beaks. They become restless when the first signs of autumn are evident. Evidently they gather in flights and travel at night, for one morning an otherwise barren marsh will be full of them. The main flights in the northern United States begin around September 1, and generally they have passed into the wintering areas in the West Indies and elsewhere by the end of October.

Soras are not fast, strong flyers. They do not rise far above the marsh grasses when flushed, and they have a habit of fluttering and circling around gunners. To a beginner at rail hunting it's a tricky maneuver, but eventually the birds be-

Clapper rail is popular with shooters in tidal marshes along the lower Atlantic seaboard. (COMMISSION OF GAME AND INLAND FISHERIES PHOTO BY J. J. SHOMON)

(CONNECTICUT STATE BOARD OF FISHERIES AND GAME PHOTO BY D. N. DEANE)

Clapper rail hunting along the Atlantic coast marshes. A light punt boat is commonly used to get through grassy areas.

come easy targets. After fattening on the succulent seeds of the swamp through late summer, they're extremely delicious on the table.

Largest of American rails is the king. It's a handsome bird with a long bill, dark-brown back and cinnamon-colored breast, and thin enough to have caused the expression "skinny as a rail." Except in certain times and places, kings never approach the abundance of soras, but like soras, they're splendid fare on the table. A king will average about seventeen inches in length and will have a two-foot wingspread.

The range of the king is smaller than the sora's. It is concentrated in the fresh-water marshes of the eastern United States, but is sometimes found west to Minnesota. It is less secretive, a more powerful flyer and consequently a more lively, harder-to-hit target.

Between the king and the sora, both in size and abundance, is the Virginia rail. In appearance it is practically a pocket-edition of the king. It is almost continent-wide in distribution, and prefers fresh-water bogs and wetlands.

The best-known rail hunting is for the clappers in Atlantic salt-water areas. The bird is darker in color and only slightly smaller than the king, and its range is very limited to a thin strip along the east and west coasts. Despite food habits which tend to animals (fiddlers, shrimp, crabs, mollusks, insects) rather than vegetable materials, it is also a highly regarded table game bird. The clapper's flight is probably the strongest of all rails, but still the bird is an easy target.

Rail hunting can be extremely difficult or extremely easy, depending mostly on water levels. Generally the fresh-water rails prefer the shallowest water areas, and so it's necessary to hunt them on foot. Since the cover is invariably dense and the going slow, as in any marsh, hunting soon can get to be a rugged business. It is not always easy to flush the birds, either, because kings and soras can more easily escape by running through or under the marsh grass than by flying over it— so in most cases a close-working dog is a valuable accessory.

Pointing dogs have little value in rail hunting.

(EDUCATION DIVISION, COMMISSION OF GAME AND INLAND FISHERIES)

I've seen springer and cocker spaniels that worked well ahead of a gunner, but they're short-legged and soon fatigue in working the heavy vegetation. Robust retrievers such as Labradors and goldens are the best of all, to retrieve game as well as to flush it. A winged or crippled bird nearly always escapes without a dog, because of the nature of the cover and because the bird can swim or dive.

One reason rail hunting isn't as popular as it might be is the uncertainty of their flights. At least, hunters aren't always able to find the birds. Actually it isn't too difficult, for there are a number of ways to discover with reasonable accuracy just when and where the birds will enter any locality.

Local open seasons partially pinpoint the peaks of rail and gallinule flights. These seasons begin early everywhere and they're calculated to be open during the main flight in any region. Opening day, for example, is set to allow for a very early flight, and closing day (usually more than two months later) for an extremely late flight. The main flight is figured to arrive during the middle of the season. All rails are very sensitive to weather, falling temperatures and frosts. Any of these can start moving the birds southward. It's a wise sportsman who watches for noticeable weather changes just to the north of him.

Nearly every state conservation department has a migratory-bird or waterfowl biologist, and this man better than most knows pretty well when flights occur or are expected. Local bird watchers and ornithologists also keep pretty close track of these movements, and are accurate sources of information. It's a good idea to contact them. The charts with this chapter also show approximate dates of arrival. But the most positive method is to make a personal reconnaissance. You'll also learn plenty about other marsh critters—about the ducks and geese—for hunting seasons later on.

Occasionally special situations—such as the rice or millet harvest in the lower Mississippi Valley—will concentrate the birds enough to make hunting on foot a relatively leisurely pastime, but that's too seldom the case. Usually it's a matter of slogging the heaviest cover, through cattails, smartweed and the like, to put birds in the air. Try to concentrate on areas of vegetation heavy with seeds. This is rough going when the weather is warm, but it will put game in the bag and your legs in shape for upland season later on.

Concentrate on the edges of marshes. Usually the weeds here grow especially lush, and it's no picnic to wade through them. But it's precisely here that the most rails will be. Never pass up the small islands or fingers of land in marshes, nor the weedy edges of dikes, fills and embankments. The upper, shallow sections of reservoirs and headwater lakes are always favorite stopovers for rails, especially for soras; so are the swampy flats created by beaver workings. Farm ponds sometimes attract them. Obviously several hunters can be more successful by walking abreast quickly through such cover because the birds can elude a single hunter more easily.

Veterans of marsh-hen hunting use a couple of tricks that save plenty of steps in a season of hunting. First they listen for the birds to spot concentrations of them. Rails give a harsh, somewhat strident *yick, yick, yick* call that is invariably answered by other rails. Of course, it's a dead giveaway to their location once a hunter learns to identify the call. It takes some experience, though, because a marsh produces many similar sounds.

Another old trick is to circle and test suitable cover by tossing sticks or clods of earth into it. When something falls nearby, a rail will usually call in alarm, and again other rails will answer.

Since the best rail hunting occurs in warm weather and over wet ground, it's best to dress lightly for the most comfort. It's hard to beat a cotton khaki shirt and trousers. Most hunters prefer to tramp the marshes "wet"—with cotton socks and tennis shoes—but nowadays there are plenty of extra-lightweight waders on the market. The best shooting is early in the morning, for several reasons. It's cooler, the rails are more active, they call more frequently and the entire marsh is more "alive" at this time.

The most ideal condition exists on a high tide, when it's possible to hunt rails from a boat—as along the Atlantic coast. Of course, it's also possible in fresh-water marshes crisscrossed with channels or other waterways. Here it can actually be a leisurely, almost lazy, sport for the gunner. Any canoe or shallow-draft boat might be used, but the best craft is the old punt boat used by generations of eastern clapper hunters. Great Lakes duckboats, similar in construction, also do the job. In both of these, the gunner sits or stands in the bow while the boatman poles the boat from the stern.

Seaboard sportsmen keep a weather eye peeled for a high tide combined with a steady inshore wind. This combination floods vast areas of marsh seldom covered otherwise, and it permits a boat to weave in and out of patches of vegetation, flushing birds that are concentrated in a smaller area. Where the vegetation is most dense, the boatman uses his push-pole to "pat the lettuce," to flush birds as much as to move the boat. It all amounts to splendid sport, for a rail swinging with a brisk wind becomes a difficult target.

A good many rails come to bag when hunters work the sloughs, cuts and channels of fresh-wa-ter wetlands. Sometimes it's possible to mix boat hunting with walking, or to hunt from a boat while a retriever beats the heavy cover on the bank. Occasionally it's even possible to find these birds in numbers on bare mud flats. To tell the truth, rail hunting has endless possibilities for a sportsman who wants a full calendar afield.

Gallinules are seldom as plentiful as rails, but they're also available during long seasons and they are probably better flyers. Two species—Floridas, which are plentiful and distributed almost nationwide, and purples, which are restricted to the south—frequent approximately the same cover as rails. They prefer a little more water with their weeds, though, and they swim more often and more expertly than rails.

The best scatter-gun for marsh-hen shooting is

Gallinule also furnishes a limited amount of shooting each fall. (PHOTO BY KARL H. MASLOWSKI)

the smallest—the .410. The birds are fragile, they rarely flush at long range, they're not fast and it doesn't take a heavy load to collect them. The only gun once permitted in an old rail-shooting club on the New Jersey coast was a single-shot .410, and that's agreeable with most addicts of the sport. Although any shotgun will be suitable, especially to tune up for upland hunting, it isn't *necessary* to use anything bigger than a .410. The fact is it's possible to use a .22 rifle with dust shot where only sora shooting is involved. The .22 is much too light for the other rails and gallinules, though.

Besides a day in the field during the most elegant time of year, rail hunting offers one more bonus to American sportsmen—distinctively delicious meat for the table. The birds are small and sometimes it may seem a chore to dress them, but it's surely worth the effort. Here's a recipe to try:

Broiled Rail. Peel the birds by removing the heads, slitting down the backs and completely skinning them. Cut off the breast portion and discard the rest. Prepare a liquor of vinegar and melted butter in which a kernel of garlic has been finely ground. With it, baste the breasts liberally and place them over a small bed of charcoal. Be careful not to place them too close to the heat. Turn the birds often for five or six minutes, depending on their size, and baste each time. Served with cornbread and a green salad, they're the finest recommendation for marsh-hen hunting anyone can offer.

For every serious sportsman, there are certain days afield more memorable than all the rest. One of mine occurred early in October on the Albany River delta in far northern Ontario.

Lou Klewer and I were hunting geese on a morning when blue geese flew so fast and furiously that we needed less than an hour to bag a couple of limits. But that isn't my story. While Willie Wesley, our Cree caller, collected the decoys and the dead geese, Lou and I strolled out across the grassy tundra, which now seemed like liquid, flowing gold in the arctic wind. We hadn't walked very far before we found the grass was full of jacksnipe. They flushed ahead of us and from almost underfoot in unbelievable numbers.

"I never saw so many. . . ." Lou began.

"Let's go back and get the guns," I interrupted.

It's possible we set a new record for the quarter mile, at least on a soggy track, back to our goose blind. Then with pockets full of shells we started walking again.

A few old-time hunters will know what happened next. We enjoyed the kind of crazy, steady shooting which doesn't exist any more except in lonely, out-of-the-way places like this one. We had shots at singles and we had shots at doubles. We even had covey shots. Birds flushed ahead of us and they flushed behind. That cover was simply loaded with snipe and they boiled up and out of it at every conceivable angle. Some would fly low, barely skimming the tips of waving grass, but others would zoom upward, catch a gust of wind and then disappear a mile a minute toward the horizon.

Until I settled down, my shooting was a study in futility. My trail was marked by a long string of empty shell cases. I missed seven straight snipe before I finally tumbled a crossing shot. Then right away Lou scored a double and we began to do a little better. Still we had collected only a dozen birds before my shells—almost two boxes of them—finally ran out.

"I'm finished," I shouted to Lou, turning my pockets inside out.

"I still have two more," Lou answered, and then proceeded to miss the next two flushing snipe.

Let me say that it isn't customary for Lou to miss two consecutive shots at anything. Around Toledo, Ohio, where he's outdoor editor of the *Blade,* he has a reputation as a fine wing shot. But it's typical for jacksnipe to make monkeys of the best wing shots, because here is one of the greatest game birds on the face of the earth. For my money, the snipe is one of the toughest targets of all, a target which too few sportsmen even know about.

In camp that night, cleaning his side-by-side double with a silicone cloth, Lou said, "Let's skip the goose shooting in the morning and try those snipe instead."

He was practically reading my mind.

It wasn't long after daybreak before Lou and I were following a thin trail through the tall willows that sheltered our tent camp and bordered the Albany River in a few isolated places. A raw and icy wind whined in the treetops above us, and when we broke out into the open tundra, it

The jacksnipe, locally abundant at times, is a really great game bird. (PHOTO BY
KARL H. MASLOWSKI)

was squarely in our faces. For a mile or more we
fought the wind, shivering and hunting over the
same ground that had been alive with snipe the
day before. But now the cover was empty; we
didn't flush a single bird. The hard ground and
the crisp grass told the story. As soon as the tundra froze fast, the birds vanished silently into the
night, no doubt to begin the first lap of the long
migration southward to points unknown.

The jacksnipe, or Wilson's snipe, is surely one

of the most interesting citizens of the world.
Our American species is called Wilson's snipe
because an ornithologist named Alexander Wilson first noticed that it was slightly different
from the European snipe. But these differences
are very minor.

Any jacksnipe is a widely traveled bird. The
breeding range of the species includes the entire northern half of the United States, but no
doubt most nesting is concentrated in Canada.

Nests have been located in strange and lonely regions of the remote north, on arctic islands, in rocky Newfoundland, at Ungava, or within sound of the surf in Alaska. Snipe live and raise families in these bleak surroundings until fall and the first freeze drives them southward. Snipe must feed by probing into the soft earth with long bills for worms and other edibles, and a frozen sod makes this impossible.

Snipe migrations are as unpredictable as the weather but it's safe to say that virtually all of them winter south of the frost line. One exception would include the occasional birds which are seen around the hot springs and geyser basins of Yellowstone Park during January. Nearly all prefer Florida and the Gulf states, the West Indies, Central America and northern South America. I've had great success hunting them late in the year on the tide flats of Matanzas Bay below St. Augustine, Florida, and I have seen a few while hunting teal in Costa Rica.

An adult Wilson's snipe is handsome or ungainly, depending on how you view the long bill and long legs. His back is a rich brown, his breast a lighter brown, and his belly white. He appears to be frail, and could be mistaken in flight for such shore birds as the yellowlegs, the plover or even the dowitcher. None of these, however, has the same exciting, erratic flight so difficult to follow over a gun barrel.

Hunting jacksnipe in grasslands along James Bay, Ontario.

A generation or two ago, before the turn of the century, Wilson's snipe were exceedingly abundant. Probably in those times more snipe were shot by market hunters and by sportsmen alike than any other game birds. Although there was little excuse for his excessive slaughter, even in those days of abundance, the shooting records of one James J. Pringle of Louisiana are interesting to note.

During the twenty years from 1867 to 1887 on his favorite hunting grounds, Pringle shot a total of 69,087 snipe! But his shooting fell off woefully in the next ten years and he raised his total to only 78,603. His best day, and undoubtedly a world record—but a shameful one—was December 11, 1887, when he shot 366 snipe in six hours. That's better than one a minute! On his best seven consecutive shooting days, alternate days in December 1877, he bagged 1943 snipe. During the winter of 1874–75 he killed 6615 snipe.

At least one thing can be said for shooter Pringle: he was a great wing shot. He wrote: "I shot with only one gun at a time; had no loader, but loaded my gun myself; had I shot with two guns and had a loader I would, of course, have killed a great many more birds, but in those days and in those parts it was impossible to get a man that could be trusted to load."

Another famous gunner, Captain Bogardus, who had built a reputation on passenger pigeons and on trapshooting, also killed many snipe. One day in Illinois he bagged 340, which is only slightly behind Pringle's one-day mark. Bogardus seldom left the field without at least 150 snipe in the bag.

Even under the most perfect conditions, modern hunters can never again expect to find such concentrations of snipe in the wetlands. Although shooting once accounted for a terrible toll, it was the gradual change or destruction of habitat both on summering and wintering grounds that caused the population to decline to its present numbers. Still there are quite a few snipe on the flyways today, and with sensible bag limits and open seasons, there will always be enough of them to furnish at least a limited amount of shooting. It would be a tragedy if ever these grand game birds disappeared altogether.

There's one final word to be said about snipe: They are delicious on the table. Actually any recipe which is suitable for quail is also suitable here. But I have a favorite.

Snipe. Braise the whole birds in hot vegetable oil in a skillet. Now add salt, pepper, sour cream and dry red wine, and cook them for no more than thirty minutes. Served with a green salad, cornbread and cool ale, there's nothing—absolutely nothing—to match them on a happy autumn evening.

Pair of common coot. These birds furnish limited shooting at times to water-fowlers.

BASIC DUCK HUNTING

It was barely breaking day when Frank Sayers and I arrived at his Portage River marsh on a typical windy November morning. We parked his station wagon, shouldered a couple of sacks of decoys and followed a trail to the shooting area atop a muddy dike. We were late this morning; ordinarily we would have been in the blind an hour before, but a flat tire had caused the delay.

Halfway to the shooting hole, Frank stopped short and instantly dropped to his knees. I followed suit. Then by crawling forward on hands and knees, I saw what caused the sudden strange behavior. Maybe as many as a hundred mixed black ducks and baldpates were sitting unalarmed on the marsh.

It was a cinch for a stalking job. We could crawl to point-blank range on the opposite side of the dike. Nothing to it at all.

"Let's try them," I whispered to Frank.

"No," Frank answered, "let's just chase them away!"

If you believe that a bird in the hand is worth two somewhere else, my friend's strategy will resemble madness. But Frank knew what he was doing when he walked nonchalantly on down the dike and watched the birds wing away. Thirty minutes later our decoys were on the water, the two of us were settled in the blind and . . . in twos, threes and small flocks the ducks began filtering back. They furnished consistent shooting and it wasn't long until we had collected limits and were picking up the decoys to go home.

Of course, it doesn't always work so perfectly, but Frank was playing the odds. If we had shot the birds on the flush, our best possible bag would have been two birds each. That's good enough. But the rest of the birds would have been spooked permanently.

Nine times in ten it's better to allow the birds to make an orderly escape. Whatever attracted them there in the first place will attract them again. If not unduly frightened, they will soon return. Of course, it's terribly hard to resist at times, but the wisest duck hunter is the man who makes it a rule never to shoot at large flocks of ducks, no matter how he encounters them.

As in any other kind of hunting, success is much a matter of knowing the critter you are hunting. If you understand ducks and the instincts which govern their movements, you can be a much better (and more interested) duck hunter. First let's examine the basic movements of North American ducks, because it's so important to understand these travels.

In 1935 government biologist Frederick Lincoln and his associates made a more thorough analysis than had ever been made before of the several thousand waterfowl band returns on hand. In other words, they assembled all the data available from previous banding of waterfowl and the returns of those bands, mostly by hunters. For example, if a bird was banded in Manitoba and its band was recovered by a hunter in South Carolina, they had some idea of the bird's travel. With thousands of such records on hand, it became apparent that North American waterfowl could be separated into four separate flyways—known today as the Atlantic, Mississippi, Central or Plains, and Pacific fly-

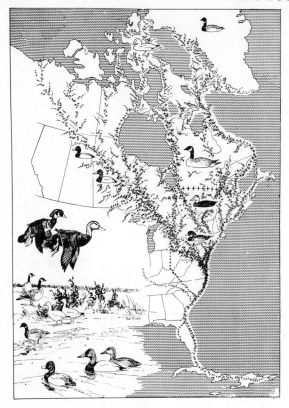

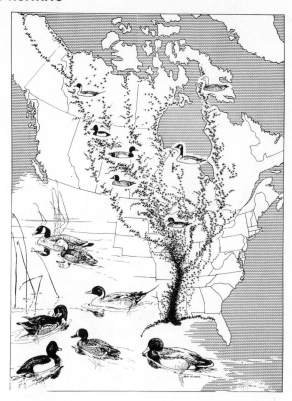

The Atlantic Flyway (U. S. FISH AND WILDLIFE SERVICE)

The Mississippi Flyway (U. S. FISH AND WILDLIFE SERVICE)

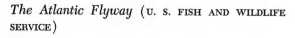

ways. Waterfowl-hunting regulations are now formulated on a flyway basis. If one species becomes scarce in one flyway, shooting will be prohibited there although it may be legal to hunt the species elsewhere.

Duck hunters and waterfowl biologists often use the terms flyway and migration routes. This is a good time to explain the difference between them. A flyway is a vast geographic region with its own breeding area and wintering grounds. The two widely separated places are connected by a system of migration routes. In other words a certain species will follow a certain migration route within its flyway when traveling from breeding to wintering areas in the fall. With

only a few exceptions, they return northward by the same routes in the springtime.

Each flyway has its own populations of waterfowl, even of species that are distributed completely across the continent or around the world. Of course, the breeding grounds of more than one flyway greatly overlap, and during the nesting season large areas are occupied by birds of the same species but of different flyways. The flyway maps in this chapter will explain more of this in detail.

Many veteran waterfowlers will find it hard to believe, but the state of the weather has far less to do with the migrations of birds than is commonly believed. I have known old duck-

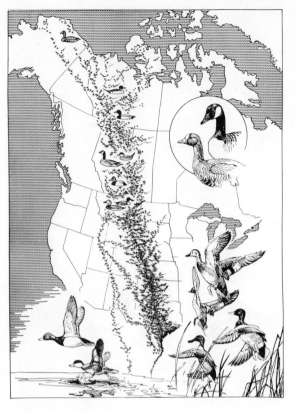

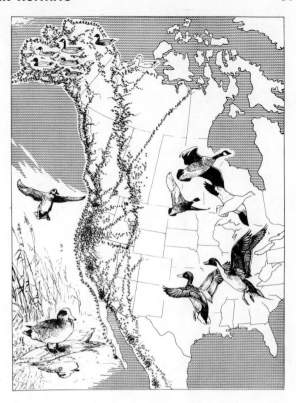

The Central Flyway (U. S. FISH AND WILDLIFE SERVICE)

The Pacific Flyway (U. S. FISH AND WILDLIFE SERVICE)

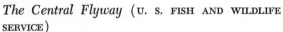

hunting guides who felt they could predict the arrival of certain duck species by consulting a barometer and the long-range weather prediction. But any successful predictions are likely to be coincidental.

According to most waterfowl biologists, migrations begin and end in obedience to mysterious physiological promptings and have no relation to prevailing weather conditions. Of course, a severe storm or a sudden freeze may force ducks to move elsewhere, possibly farther south to survive. But annual migrations are a vital part of a wild duck's life cycle, and they have become adjusted to correspond with major seasonal changes.

The serious waterfowler can use a knowledge of migration routes and approximate dates to his own advantage. Let's assume he lives in Central City and hunts on the Central River sloughs. Every year, as accurately as possible, he keeps a chart on the arrival dates of fresh flights of mallards or pintails or whatever. Pretty soon he has an accurate record compiled over several seasons, and a quick glance will reveal at which periods the odds for shooting are most in his favor. He can better plan his trips and also make better use of the time he has available for hunting.

For many reasons, but mostly because the ducks are inexperienced and still unsophisti-

Except that some vegetation has been cleared away for the photos, this is typical natural habitat for duck hunters anywhere. In this case the blind is a permanent wooden frame with fresh dressing of cattails added every season.

cated, the shooting is best immediately after a "fresh" flight arrives from the north. But with increased hunting pressure, the ducks soon mature and learn to avoid hunters and their devices. The more encounters with hunters, the more wary they become. Toward the tag end of the season, many ducks seem to know the brand names and serial numbers of all decoys.

There are good days to hunt ducks and there are poor ones. Every season is full of exceptions, but probably the best shooting occurs when the weather is worst—when a savage wind is howl-ing out of the north or northeast and when the temperature is in the lower ranges. It may not be a scientifically sound observation, but it seems to me that most species of ducks (the scaup are notable exceptions) do not enjoy resting on very turbulent or choppy water. When the wind freshens, the ducks become increasingly restless and eventually fly out to look for more sheltered places to spend the day. In other words they will be circulating among inshore areas where hunting is possible. It also seems to be the consensus among experienced gunners that ducks fly lower on rainy or snowy days.

It may seem a very elementary statement to experienced duck hunters, but day in and day out the shooting is best very early and late in the day. This is because of the habit of flying from resting to feeding areas and back again at these two periods. I have enjoyed good shooting at high noon, but only rarely. It's better to spend middays elsewhere than in a cold blind. Take a nap, burn up some ammo on clay pigeons or make a reconnaissance to see where the ducks are resting.

A session or two with the clay targets is great practice for any duck hunter, both before and during the open season. With a hand trap and a couple of cases of "birds," Frank Sayers and I toss all conceivable angles for the other to shoot. The crossing shots so common in duck hunting can be easily duplicated by tossing the clay targets directly across in front of the shooter. Overhead shots, both from behind and from the front, can also be duplicated by standing behind and higher than the shooter or in defilade in front of him.

We've duplicated the high passing shots of ducks by tossing targets out the second floor window of an old barn. We have also practiced shooting from a sitting position, a highly valuable drill if your plans include float-tripping for ducks by boat.

If you are a member of a duck club, most of your problems are already solved. You simply make whatever reservations the club requires and then go shooting. The blinds, boats, decoys and, you hope, the ducks are waiting. But if you are a non-member, your duck hunting should begin *before* opening day—except that you leave your gun at home. Take a road map and hiking shoes instead.

The first step is to locate the ducks, and the sooner the better. Find a migration route and then find specific places along the way where ducks are loitering. Next, try to determine their habits. See where they are feeding. Try to locate specifically the routes they fly between resting and feeding areas. Finally try to locate your blind (as long before opening day as logically possible) as conveniently as terrain, legal permission and suitable water permits, to intercept the ducks somewhere or sometime during

View from blind as hunter tosses out decoys. This shows relation between blind's location and placement of stool.

Frank Sayers in pit blind on a rocky Lake Erie island. When birds approach, he ducks down low.

View from a blind on an Ohio river. Notice how ice has started to form around edges. Hunter has just bagged two blacks.

Hunter crouches lower in pit blind as approach blind.

Hunter suddenly rises up out of blind as mallard comes into close range. He is holding perfect lead on the drake.

Hunter waits near spread of decoys on a Midwestern farm pond. Good shooting often is possible in places like these.

their daily routine. But keep in mind that once heavy gunning begins, their routine may be interrupted or at least altered.

It is highly important to have clear-cut permission, preferably in writing (which is required by law in some states) before you trespass and build a blind. Laws are strange, vague and varied in many states, especially as they pertain to water and riparian rights. Make certain you know them before blundering into legal trouble.

During pre-shooting-season reconnaissance, carry good binoculars or a spotting scope. These optics are invaluable in locating resting flocks and flight lines, and will also save you making plenty of footprints across soggy real estate.

Talk to farmers when you can, or to the local game warden. He will know where waterfowl are concentrated. Sometimes rural mailmen are able to give tips on where they consistently see waterfowl during daily travels.

In most states there are public hunting areas that either were acquired especially for duck hunting or on which some duck hunting in season is possible. It's a good idea to inquire about these, and for that purpose a list of state conservation bureaus is furnished elsewhere in this volume. On many of these state areas, hunting is permitted for a low daily fee, for which a blind and boat are furnished. In other instances permits are free. Where the demand for duck-hunting space is very great, the permits are issued on a lottery basis.

In some regions where waterfowling is an important activity, blinds or hunting areas can be rented by the day or leased for longer periods of time. Finding the locations of these is a matter of inquiring locally, or checking with the game warden or other conservation officials.

One last bit of advice for the fledgling duck hunter. Besides a valid state hunting license, you will need a current Migratory Waterfowl Stamp before hunting anywhere in the United States. These cost three dollars and can be purchased in any post office. Revenue from sale of the stamps is used in scientific waterfowl management and to acquire wetlands on which waterfowl can live. In other words, you are contributing to better waterfowling in the future when you purchase your stamp.

Chapter 7

DUCK BLINDS

It isn't often that a wind becomes as raw and penetrating as one did on a December morning at Tennessee's Reelfoot Lake, although this was only a couple of good casts from the cotton fields. Nor have I often seen such unusual shooting, because I stood in full view of a constant stream of canvasbacks that roared downwind to reach the stool and the patch of buffalo grass just below me.

The canvasbacks poured in crazily, some close enough for me to feel the rush of wings. It happened that I was standing about fifteen feet above the water. My blind was merely a small platform—standing room—atop the sawed-off

Among the simplest of the pit blinds is a sunken vinegar or beer barrel. Most popular in the plains states, it works well in many situations because the waterfowler is completely concealed. Holes should be drilled in the bottom of the barrel and a layer of rocks placed just beneath it for drainage if the bottom is above water level. The barrel can be kept covered when not in use.

This is a semi-permanent movable blind mostly for river shooting. The wooden frame is mounted on skids and the exterior is covered with native willow or grass. The blind can be moved to new locations as water levels or flight patterns change. This particular blind is located on a Mississippi sandbar near New Madrid, Missouri.

Since waterfowl often move on to feed in other fields after a session of shooting, a movable blind like this one, constructed to resemble a corn shock, is useful. The gunner can just pick up the blind and walk away. Or he can leave the blind in position while he goes elsewhere.

trunk of a cypress tree. To the decoying ducks I guess I resembled part of the tree trunk, and the surrounding limbs were enough to break up any telltale silhouette. I've enjoyed much more comfortable blinds, but not too many which were more unusual or more effective.

A good part of waterfowling success anywhere is the hunter's ability to conceal himself. Ducks and geese have extraordinary vision, and they rate with America's most shy and wary wildlife. They seldom come into shotgun range unless the hunter is hidden or sufficiently disguised.

Although building a blind can be a challenge to a sportsman's ingenuity, it is no complicated matter. Ordinarily there are enough natural materials everywhere for the construction. It is up to the hunter to make the best use of these materials, and he should remember that deception is the most vital part of his work. Here is how Frank Vorhees and I solved a typical problem early one season when we spotted a concentration of wood ducks and teal in a pond-and-pothole section in Delaware County in Ohio.

Before the season opened Frank had found an oxbow of a relocated creek where the ducks seemed to loiter for many hours during the day. He placed our blind in the center of the oxbow and on the inside of the curve. The framework was fashioned from saplings, which he cut near the site. Since the slopes surrounding the oxbow were dotted with scarlet sumac, Frank cut pieces of this plant at random and lashed them to his frame until it resembled another clump of sumac. For several days, until a cold front pushed the bluewings and the wood ducks farther south, we had memorable shooting.

A blind can be a fairly permanent structure or it can be only temporary, depending on its

This is the type of blind a hunter would expect to find at goose hunting clubs near Horseshoe Lake, Illinois, and elsewhere that goose shooting is very popular. There is a bench inside on which the hunters can sit in comfort. A carefully camouflaged top slides forward to allow hunters to shoot as geese decoy close.

location. In the marsh or swampy sections along established flyways a permanent blind is more economical. Where the habits of ducks are not stable, or perhaps just for a one-time shoot, a temporary blind is enough. But for either type, the blind builder must always keep some important considerations in mind.

The first is the prevailing wind and the flight pattern of the ducks. If they ordinarily approach from one direction, the blind should face that way to give the best field of fire. The exact location of the blind is important too, from the standpoint of access in all sorts of weather. When water levels fall, it's sometimes impossible to hike across miles of mud flats that were easily negotiated by boat before. This is a common problem when hunting ducks in tidal areas. One word to the wise waterfowler. Points of land are nearly always good if they are accessible.

Camouflage is next in importance to placement of the blind. The surrounding scene or landscape should be changed as little as possi-

ble. And that means using local materials, a point which cannot be stressed too much. It's good advice to avoid using materials which stand out like sore thumbs—which clash with the environment—such as green lumber in a permanent marsh blind. It is far better to use scrap or weathered lumber.

When using local grasses and foliage, be certain to gather it some distance away from the blind. And at the same time be sure to duplicate the nearby material so that the immediate area of your blind has no tramped-down or cut-over look. These considerations become much more important as the duck season progresses and the ducks become more sophisticated.

I have found that certain materials, tools and equipment are so handy in blind building that I would advise the wandering waterfowler to carry them in his car trunk at all times during the fall. These items include a hand ax, an infantry shovel, baling wire, Manila twine, burlap sacking and staples. With these a man can quickly and easily erect a temporary blind almost anywhere.

Chicken wire and three-foot wire garden fencing are extremely valuable too. One duck hunter I know weaves marsh grass into a twelve-foot section of garden wire. All through the season he carries it rolled up in his station wagon. In a few minutes' time he can set up this blind for business just by unrolling the wire and forcing the ends of it into the soft ground.

Many good duck-hunting areas are located near waters where commercial fishing is carried on, and this means that fish netting is available. Old and weathered fish netting is a splendid blind material. Spread it across a frame and then weave grass, foliage, or strips of burlap into the net. It is a good idea to take the netting down after every session in the blind, because in bad weather it is easily blown away.

Remember that burlap is also an extremely good camouflage material. It is excellent for covering the blind and it is also very handy in making a duck hunter's uniform. Sheets of burlap can be sewed together to form an outer garment that is easily concealed among natural foliage. Strips of burlap inside a blind also give some insulation and add warmth on bad days.

Along rocky shores and jetties, piled-up rocks can make a natural and effective blind. The

On such open waters as on North Carolina's Pamlico Sound, a floating blind can be a deadly duck producer. The rig is easily moved to new spots simply by cranking up the outboard, but it cannot be anchored very far from shore. The outboard is perfectly legal in most states if it is tipped up during actual shooting. Nor can an outboard be used to follow or to flush ducks.

These photos show how native grasses can be fashioned to form a light and portable blind. Grasses are woven to heavy cord to form a mat and the mat is rolled up. It can be carried in a station wagon and placed almost anywhere near the water's edge to form a good camouflaged position for the duck hunter.

A blind made of light wood framing and white sheet used for shooting on the ice, beside open water, late in the season. This one is in use on Sandusky Bay in Ohio.

This hunter is crouched inside a blind on the Mississippi River near Reelfoot Lake, Tennessee. The burlap material is not only good camouflage but furnishes a certain amount of insulation in this extremely cold spot on a windy day. Notice the small homemade wood and coal stove.

hunter can hide behind them or build a four-wall pit which offers protection as well as concealment. Often it is a good idea first to build a framework, perhaps of old wooden timbers or driftwood, and then to pile the rocks roughly around the outside as a stone mason might do. This type of blind is extremely effective around the rocky islands of Lake Erie, and no doubt it would be equally as suitable in similar areas elsewhere.

Comfort is important for spending long hours in a blind. But camouflage should be the first consideration. It is a wise waterfowler who keeps the vicinity of his blind policed of empty cigarette packages, sandwich wrappers, empty shell cases and other litter that will seem unnatural to a passing duck.

The size of any blind is very important. A space about three feet square will accommodate any but the largest man. A two-man blind, sunken or above water, should be about six feet by three feet and about four feet high. The average man is comfortable on a seat eighteen inches high.

Wherever the location will permit, pit or sunken blinds are at least as effective as any built above ground. Depending upon situation and permanence, they can be for standing, sitting or prone shooting. They can be simple earth excavations or they can be made from

This blind, in Maryland, is a typical duck blind design all over the United States. The wooden framework is permanent and is large enough so that two hunters can sit comfortably for long periods of time. Only the outer dressing of grass or cornstalks must be replaced every year.

This Florida hunter who is watching for mallards to descend on this cluttered oak forest has camouflaged himself with Spanish moss, a natural material very abundant in the area.

These hunters have remembered to take utmost advantage of natural cover by using these cypress trees at Tennessee's Reelfoot Lake as blinds. Platforms are built inside the trees or on top of the stumps. The motionless hunter blends into the tree trunk and resembles another dead limb. Ducks in the area have grown accustomed to these cypress "ghosts" and unless the hunter makes unnecessary moves, he will not be spotted too easily.

sunken barrels. Where drainage is no problem, they can be lined inside with concrete blocks. The covers or lids can be anything from cornstalks to mats of woven grass to cemetery cloth. The hunter shoots from a sitting position or throws off the lid and jumps up to shoot.

Sunken blinds are the most effective where the land or terrain is flat, such as in grainfields from which the grain has been harvested.

A sunken barrel can be located in open water as well as on dry land. But there is a trick to doing it. The barrel is filled with water to sink it and is fastened to stakes driven into the bottom beside it. Then the barrel is pumped dry.

As I pointed out before, only the ingenuity of an outdoorsman limits the potential of effective blind building. Some gunners I've known have even planted and grown their own blinds. One waterfowler I knew in Mississippi erected a permanent blind and then transplanted honeysuckle, an evergreen plant, all around it. The honeysuckle grew and enveloped the blind. The hunter needed only to trim out a small shooting space at the beginning of each season.

In Florida I knew another sportsman who sawed off five feet above water line a large cy-

This is a one-of-a-kind blind built from mirrors and used at Remington Farms in Maryland. The geese standing beside the blind are mounted birds. Although it is as much a novelty as a practical blind, it is said to be devastatingly effective on dull days.

press that had been killed by lightning many years before. It was already partially decayed and hollowed out, so the man only whittled away until he had enough space to sit inside, almost completely hidden. Many an unsuspecting pintail and mallard was bagged from that stump during the seasons which followed.

And then there are floating blinds. Many of those we've mentioned so far can be mounted on steel oil drums or pontoons and anchored wherever ducks are flying. An alternative to the floating blind is the stake blind, which the hunter can build by cutting saplings and arranging them in a circle in the water. The hunter then stands hidden in the center of the circle. Of course, hip boots or waders are necessary for this type of structure.

Sometimes it may be necessary to use a boat as a blind, because there are circumstances where this method cannot be avoided. However, there are drawbacks, and the main one is the lack of concealment from above. Another is the element of danger when two gunners use the same boat. If you do use a boat for tidewater shooting, be sure that you have reliable information on tides.

It has been the unhappy experience of many gunners to find the perfect spot among the reeds with only a foot or two of water, and then to have the tide run out. That could mean spending a cold and miserable six to eight hours or more waiting for the tide to come in again, before it is possible to move the boat to open water.

The use of a boat for a blind is far more acceptable on fresh-water lakes where water levels do not fluctuate. On many rivers the boat can be successfully concealed beneath overhanging trees or alders. Elsewhere the boat can be camouflaged with natural material gathered nearby on the bank. An inverted boat can also

This hunter uses an old wooden beer case as a handy seat inside his blind. The compartments in the beer case hold a duck and a goose call, shells, cigarettes, and matches. A thermos jug of hot beverage will come in handy when a raw wind begins to blow.

Typical of the manufactured blinds now available on the market is this one-man model in which chicken wire is the base material. Native weeds or grasses are woven through the wire mesh. It can be used on land or water. (PHOTO BY THE PORTA COMPANY, INC., CANTON, MASS.)

be used; Glenn Lau and I have done this while "laying out" for ducks and geese on small reefs and rock piles in Lake Erie.

In recent years a number of manufactured portable blinds have appeared on the market, and they are filling an important niche for duck hunters. A collapsible canvas blind can be a valuable addition to the wandering duck hunter's gear. A portable cornstalk blind can be very helpful to the grainfield shooter.

Any blind should be built as long as possible before you plan to use it. This is particularly true of a permanent blind. This gives waterfowl a chance to get used to it and accept it as part of the scene.

This much is certain, no duck hunt can be very successful unless the duck hunter is hidden. And how well he is hidden depends upon where, when and how well he has built his blind.

Chapter 8

WATERFOWL DECOYS

A thousand years ago in the southwest, an Indian sat in a cave and fashioned a counterfeit canvasback duck. He formed the head and body of reeds, bound them tightly with bulrushes, and colored them with pigments. Finally he stuck feathers into the body to make it as lifelike as possible.

The finished product was what is now the world's oldest known waterfowl decoy. It was discovered in Lovelock Cave, Nevada, in 1924. Today anybody can see it in New York's Museum of the American Indian.

Similar reed counterfeits attracted wild ducks into the range of primitive Indian weapons—throw nets or bows and arrows—and decoys have been in use ever since. Only the design and the materials have changed: from reeds, mud and skins, to wood and modern plastics. But no matter what the material, decoys are almost as important to duck hunters today as their guns.

The story of decoys and decoy-making has all the romance and color of the history of America. There is a close parallel, in fact, because waterfowling is a traditional sport. Settlers in the seventeenth century were faced with an endless search for food. The decoys they copied from the Indians made the search a bit easier. But the reed and duckskin decoys blew away during bad weather (when waterfowling is often best), and some anonymous settler began whittling wooden decoys in what little spare time was available.

The first whittled models were merely rough wooden affairs in the general shape of swimming ducks. They were called blocks or stools, the latter from "stool pigeon," a device long used to

attract and trap pigeons in the Old World. The word *decoy* didn't come into use until after 1800; it comes from the contraction of Dutch words which mean duck cage or trap.

In the early days of settlement on the eastern seaboard, waterfowl were less sophisticated than they are today. Young birds especially would

Glenn Lau shows how to set up dead Canada goose for use as decoy.

drop in to decoys which only remotely resembled live ducks. As hunting increased and the ducks got smarter, better decoys were needed. One result was that decoy-making became a specialized craft and some decoy-makers became artists in the truest sense of the word. Not only were the body shapes true and graceful, but each decoy was carefully painted. Today some of their original decoys are as valuable as the best of early American paintings.

By 1850 or thereabouts, decoy-making was a recognized and highly important profession. A single hunter might use as many as five hundred decoys, and there are records of even larger "spreads" in the Susquehanna River flats and in Chesapeake Bay. Definite regional types also began to appear.

The Stratford and Housatonic River area of Connecticut became known for uniformly fine, exquisite decoys. Barnegat Bay decoys were hollow (and therefore lighter), so that a hunter could carry more of them. Miniature models appeared in portions of New England; the small size was less conspicuous and less likely to betray

These show the effective manner in which old auto tires can be converted into excellent decoys for Canada geese and snow geese. These are used on the sandbars of Nebraska rivers, but would be good elsewhere, too. (NEBRASKA GAME COMMISSION PHOTOS BY GENE HORNBECK)

hunters who violated laws against Sunday shooting.

Decoy-making wasn't confined to ducks alone. Some craftsmen specialized in geese, both in building full-bodied, full-size models and in making the silhouette decoys which are still used today. In addition there were swan, curlew, rail, dowitcher, plover, coot, snipe and heron decoys. A number of very old, quaint loon decoys are in existence. So are gull stools, but these are considered "confidence decoys" rather than an attempt to entice gulls in to gunning range. The

theory was that swimming gulls gave circling ducks enough confidence to come closer.

The end of the nineteenth century marked the greatest era of wildfowl gunning ever known on earth. Besides the sportsmen, market hunters were operating everywhere, and the need for decoys was immense. Even though live ducks were being used as stools, the demand for artificials was so great that factories rather than individual artists began to produce most of them.

During the Civil War the first rubber decoy appeared. Soon after, a quacking decoy was pat-

Showing construction of sturdy, durable cork decoys for puddle ducks.

Comparison of manufactured goose decoys with a mounted bird, also a decoy. These are made of plastic, wood, cork, papier-mâché.

ented. The quacking was caused by a bellows worked by wave action. Still later came tip-up decoys, operated with strings or pulleys, to simulate ducks feeding on the surface. Someone began to use cork instead of cedar, the standard material.

Nowadays, with waterfowl at only a fraction of their abundance of half a century ago, most decoys are mass produced of plastic, papier-mâché, or similar inexpensive materials. Of course they're just as attractive (perhaps more so to ducks) and more durable than the old hand-crafted models. But they lack the character of decoys handmade in the hickory-smoked past. Duck hunters of an older generation understand this best.

But make no mistake, old duck decoys are vastly more valuable today than ever before. Prices of some run into four figures. Many antique collectors specialize in waterfowl stools, and there is great competition to acquire the "old masters." Among the greatest, "most wanted" makers are Charles "Shang" Wheeler, Joel Barber and Albert Laing of Connecticut, Henry Perdew of Illinois, John Blair of Philadelphia, Jason Dodge of Detroit and George Warren of Toronto.

And there are many, many others.

Antique-decoy collectors ply their hobbies in numerous ways and places. They frequent auctions, rummages, and sales of large estates. If the estate owners were known to be waterfowlers, the word spreads and collectors gather from far away. Perhaps the most fertile hunting grounds are around old duck-hunting clubs (some famous, but some long ago dissolved) in nearby barns and attics. So keen has the collecting become that it's hard to say which is more exciting, actually hunting ducks with decoys or just finding a rare old block somewhere.

Antique decoys are in great demand to decorate dens and living rooms, offices and hunting lodges. Homemakers use them as centerpieces and in flower arrangements.

Today's decoys, manufactured of everything from plastic and rubber to polyurethane and papier-mâché, aren't nearly so elegant as yesterday's handmade cork and cedar counterfeits, which now are more valuable as collectors items than as decoys. The modern decoys are much easier to transport in quantity.

An example of the extremes to which a serious sportsman will go to enjoy good goose hunting was Glenn L. Martin, a pioneer in American aviation who hunted geese in the grand style and with the ultimate in decoys. After use of live decoys was outlawed many years ago, he used only wild honkers mounted by a taxidermist in natural feeding postures. But, curiously enough, other

Details of how goose decoys can be made from chicken wire and cloth. (NEBRASKA GAME COMMISSION PHOTOS BY GENE HORNBECK)

serious goose hunters have found that silhouettes, simple goose shapes cut out of plywood, work just as well.

Many sportsmen wonder whether it is worth the time and trouble to make their own decoys either for duck or goose shooting. The answer in most cases is probably that it is. Mass-produced decoys can be sturdy, durable and even very effective, but it is impossible to match the authenticity and style which a waterfowler can produce in his own home workshop. But more than this is the satisfaction of making a counterfeit of your own which will one day attract a flock of ducks within easy shooting range. There are a number of good publications on the market today that outline in detail and step by step how to make decoys for all species of ducks.

The proper placement of decoys and the ar-

Duck hunter on Sandusky Bay, Ohio, uses piles of mud to supplement regular black and mallard decoys.

Goose hunter makes silhouette decoys in a basement workshop. These are easy and inexpensive to make—and effective as well.

rangement of a good stool is a subject for controversy wherever two or more duck hunters gather. Ducks are about as unpredictable as trout in heavily fished waters. To say that one type of placement will work is about like saying a certain fly will always catch trout. Trout fishermen know there is no such fly.

Let's see what it is that makes waterfowl come to artificial decoys in the first place. To begin with, they are gregarious critters and would rather be with other ducks of their own kind than alone. No doubt the sight of other ducks on the water gives assurance to approaching ducks that there is no danger below. It also might suggest to them the presence of food.

There is good evidence that the more elaborate and authentic the decoy the more readily ducks will come in to it. However, ducks and geese are known to decoy in to everything from rusty tin cans and mounds of mud to pieces of rubber tire and old cardboard boxes. In Canada, I have seen Cree Indians use sticks and mud, the skins of dead birds, dead birds propped up, and just the wings of birds fastened to sticks.

Many times a waterfowler will find himself far from a source of decoys, and it is well to remember that some of these simple items will work. As in any phase of duck hunting, ingenuity in preparing and setting out decoys can mean the difference between success and failure.

Cree Indian method of rigging a dead blue goose to use as a decoy.

Speaking of waterfowling in general, ducks and geese will decoy best to large numbers of their own kind. In other words, the more decoys on the water the better the chances of pulling in birds. A possible exception to this might be in hunting the shallow-water ducks on small

These canvasback decoys are very old and can still be used in the field. However, they're far more valuable now as collectors' items.

streams or along potholes. Also, approaching teal or wood ducks might find it far more natural if only a few ducks were previously on the pond. In hunting the diving ducks—canvasbacks, redheads and bluebills—more decoys invariably means better shooting.

Although ducks may be more susceptible to a spread of decoys simulating their own species, most ducks will decoy to unidentified species. Otherwise why would any duck ever come in close to blobs of mud or to decoys made out of cardboard boxes? Some birds not in the waterfowl family or entirely different kinds of waterfowl actually seem to give certain ducks confidence. For example, it is an old-time trick when hunting puddle ducks to include Canada geese or coot or even a few gull decoys around the fringe of the decoys. All kinds of ducks often pour into areas where there are concentrations of wild geese. They will do the same thing if there are goose decoys among the duck decoys.

No doubt a gunner's best bet is to observe wild ducks whenever he has the opportunity and see how they deport and place themselves when resting on the water. For example, feeding puddle ducks will ordinarily not bunch together unless they have been baited. They will be scattered out evenly over an area, no two ducks very close together. This, then, should be the way puddle-duck decoys are arranged before a shoot.

Among the common tricks of setting out decoys for the diving ducks is to arrange them in a pattern so that an open space exists among the decoys and this open space is within easy shooting range of the blind. The actual formation might be an oval, it might be heart-shaped or fishhook shaped. In any case, there must be ample space for new arrivals to land in the center of the blocks.

Tossing out the decoys in relation to the blind might be more important than any other factor in proper placement. Remember that nearly all ducks when making a final approach toward the decoys will come upwind. The blind therefore should be located so that a shooter can take advantage of this approach and have the best possible open shot at the approaching birds. A very common mistake is to place the decoys too far from the blind. This kind of stool is of little value because decoying ducks will settle far out of range and will either furnish the shooter with no

Skin of a drake wood duck used as a decoy on a small woodland pond.

Indian decoy of mud and sticks—but suitable in a pinch anytime when regular dekes aren't handy.

action at all or will cause him to take longer than sensible shots, which will only cripple game.

There are other little details about the placement of decoys that most experienced waterfowlers keep in mind. If it is midday, for example, and the shooting is for puddle ducks, they will always place a few individual decoys on the shore, or on dry land, because it is the habit of puddle ducks to rest in this manner. It is doubly characteristic on warm days.

Be sure that decoys are always well anchored and that at least at the beginning of the season strong new cord is used to tie between decoy and anchor. Many a valuable decoy has been lost in a strong wind or storm because last year's decayed or weakened line was used. Also, be certain that the lines are not white or bright in color, because in clear water these are telltale signs to approaching ducks that all is not well below.

To tell the truth, entire volumes could be written on the proper placement of waterfowl decoys. But it really boils down to the individual shooter's ingenuity and to his instinct for what will more quickly and more effectively attract waterfowl within shooting range. Some days the ducks will make a man feel he is truly an expert and that he has at last mastered decoy placement. On other days they will make him wish he had stayed home.

Chapter 9

FREELANCING FOR DUCKS

Occasionally, nowadays, wildfowling might seem a thing of the past for the average sportsman. Most of the best wildfowling areas—the marshes, deltas and wet lowlands on major flyways—are solidly in private ownership, as we've pointed out before.

But fortunately there is still plenty of opportunity for any enterprising scatter-gunner. It's not a cut-and-dried case of slipping into a prepared blind at daybreak and waiting for rafts of mallards to struggle upwind into a grand spread of decoys. Not at all. Nor is it sustained pass shooting where ducks are forced to funnel past a certain strategic spot from feeding to resting grounds. It's neither easy nor predictable. But it *is* productive and can be very exciting.

Take the farm ponds. There are nearly three quarters of a million of them across America's landscape today. They are so numerous in places that some biologists are suggesting they could alter age-old migration flyways. But best of all, ducks drop in on them and evidently like what they find, for they stay until they're disturbed. Getting a four-duck limit, for example, could often be a matter of properly hunting a couple of ponds. Here's how:

First obtain the landowner's permission. That's usually not difficult if you use the same courtesy and approach you use in other matters. After that, it's a test of how good an infantryman you would make if suddenly drafted into the army.

Inadvertently, of course, farm ponds were as well designed for duck hunters as they were for storing water. Typical construction places a low dam across a small shallow drainage. By ap-

proaching from downstream and keeping below the crest of the dam, perhaps by crawling and creeping, a hunter can approach to within shotgun range of the birds without ever being seen. If he's a good shot, he'll take a couple on the flush. If not, it was good practice for the next try.

A two-man team can work the farm-pond ducks just as effectively—maybe more so. While one man crawls up from the dam side, another makes a wide circle out of sight and begins a crawling stalk from the upstream side. The ducks are sandwiched and one gunner is almost certain to have action.

Crawling is an art in itself and for some of these farm ponds with very low dams, you'd better learn how. In a prone position, lay your gun across the crook in your elbow. Carry it right there. Keeping your head and buttocks down, move forward by advancing the left elbow and left knee, then your right elbow and right knee at the same time. It's slow and tedious but it's as good for sneaking up on ducks as it was for its original purpose of infiltrating enemy positions.

But that's still not the whole farm-pond story. Find a pond that's located near larger waters where ducks concentrate in great numbers and you've found a fine spot to pitch out a few blocks. Build a hasty blind and sit for a few hours early and late in the day—perhaps all day if the weather raises too rough a chop for the ducks to rest out on open water. The birds will gradually filter in to find more quiet places. That's when you can collect a few in duck-club style. Group your decoys loosely in a sheltered place.

All these are photos of floating downstream on rivers to jump-shoot ducks. Notice how the canoes and boats are camouflaged with burlap and natural material obtained on the stream banks. Notice also how hunters camouflage their faces and how they try to avoid the use of paddles and oars. The object is to try to simulate a pile of debris or driftwood floating down the river.

If you're using decoys, why not try something a little more effective than the usual motionless spread. Place a heavy anchor or weight with an "eye" in the center of the blocks. Run a Manila or hemp line from your blind, through the eye of the anchor, and tie it to the bill of a decoy floating just over the anchor. When ducks come in range, pull gently on the line, causing the block to tip up like a duck feeding. It's a real magnet, particularly when the water is calm.

There is a lot more to good duck hunting than the actual shooting. It's fascinating, even legal, to start before the season opens. Just leave your shooting iron at home and tote a pair of binoculars instead. Methodically, whenever there's a little spare time, reconnoiter every patch of water in your neighborhood where shooting might be permitted. Some flights usually arrive in every region before opening day, so make it a point to know just where they are and what they're doing. Check all the inconsequential ponds, sloughs, potholes, creeks, rivers—the works. Visit some farmers and inquire about hunting on their ponds. Get a county map (most county engineers or surveyors have them available) if necessary to locate waters you've never known about. Look especially for newly flooded woods and croplands; these are terrific.

Now it's eve of opening day. You know where the most ducks are loitering. You know which

This hunter, Mike Nauer, uses a floater bubble, waders, a camouflage suit, and a swimmer's flippers on his feet to float downstream for ducks.

Tom Henderson's Tintex pond (described in this chapter) on a central Ohio stream. Decoys are shown exactly as he arranged them on the fake pond. Henderson is crouched on the ice at the left.

place is the easiest to approach. So make your choice and be sitting there quietly when day begins to break—or at the opening hour, whenever that is in your state. You should have action soon.

It's important to be well hidden when you wait for that opening hour. But it's not difficult even without a blind. Get a couple of used feed or potato sacks, any kind as long as they're burlap or hemp. With any old paints you have around the house, daub spots of various colors over the burlap in no particular pattern to break the outline. Try to get the camouflage effect that was successful in the jungle-fighting gear of World War II. Cut a hole for your head in the

bottom of the bag and a couple of armholes on each side and you have a slipover vest that from above is hard to distinguish against the background.

Cut out the corner of another sack, give it the same paint treatment, and you have a good coolie-type hat for your head. Daub your cheeks, chin, nose and forehead with charcoal, watercolor paint or mud to eliminate "shine" and it will take a mighty wary duck to be suspicious of your form huddled far below.

Sit still, absolutely still, until action develops. Get a handwarmer or two if necessary to make you more comfortable and less restless. If the cover and vegetation around the pond is suitable,

take a small folding canvas chair, also to make being immobile more easy.

For some reason, wildfowlers seem to neglect the rivers. Perhaps it's because the ducks are hidden too well behind the bends of a meandering waterway and the impression is that no ducks are there at all. But that's rarely true, for some ducks—even geese—seem to prefer water that moves.

Certainly hunting the rivers isn't always an easy matter. If the water is low it means carrying equipment over deadfalls, around rapids and through shallow bars, and lugging a boat or canoe to and from the water. But these are small hardships for the sport a clever gunner will enjoy during a float trip.

The ideal way to hunt a river is by drifting. You put a boat in at one point and float downstream, perhaps between bridges. You can use two cars or arrange to be picked up by someone

Lon Parker spreading his polyethylene pond on a picked cornfield. Notice how he can conceal himself directly under the pond.

else at closing time. A rowboat is by far the most comfortable, but a canoe is most maneuverable and easiest to handle around obstacles. But a canoe is also less stable when shooting suddenly develops around a bend. Take your choice and proceed with care.

Few ducks will allow an uncamouflaged craft to drift close enough for a shot. So there's work to be done before shoving off. There are many ways to disguise the outline of boat and hunters (which should be the main consideration) simply by using the materials around a riverbank, plus plenty of heavy Manila cord. Cut a supply of willows, if the leaves are still on, or any native grasses growing nearby. Weave or tie this material together as densely as possible with the cord

and then completely encircle the boat or canoe with it, tying at intervals to the gunwale. When the finished product looks like a pile of brush or driftwood at a hundred feet, you're ready to start collecting the legal limit.

Drift freely as much as possible. Never use oars, and use paddles as sparingly as possible when ducks are in sight. When approaching a bend or curve in the river, stay as close as you can to the inside bank. It will give a better shot at birds suddenly flushing when you surprise them.

Here's a stratagem that often pays off when floating. Keep an eye peeled for waterfowl far ahead. As soon as you spot them, swing in to the nearest shore where one hunter can disembark.

These are pictures at Beaverhead County, Montana, of hunters jump-shooting ducks on Red Rock Creek. It is very productive hunting but it means crawling long distances on hands and knees in infantry style.

Jump-shooting on farm ponds can be highly productive and exciting. Notice how the Labrador retriever is already on his way to retrieve the duck which has been hit by the hunter standing in the high cattails.

As soon as that hunter has had time to make a wide swing to get far below the ducks you spotted, push out into the stream and begin the drift again. It's the old sandwich play, which more often than not, if he's well hidden, drives the ducks right past the hunter who made the circle on foot.

The free-lance hunter may not get as much chance at the so-called choice species of ducks as the sportsman on a private marsh or preserve. But often it's for the better. The gunner drifting on rivers more often encounters a brilliant, furtive bird—the wood duck—that many feel is far superior to any of his cousins once he's plucked and ready for the table. Same for the bluewing teal, which also keeps to sluggish rivers and to small secluded ponds. Add the tasty ruddy to the list too.

Even geese are available to the average gunner if he'll spend a little time and concentration on locating them. Canadas especially are creatures of habit. Until something interrupts them, they fall into a rut and stay there. Assume a flight of honkers has dropped into a lake near where you live. They'll probably stay until the place freezes, or until they strip the fields of grain, or until the pressure of hunters becomes too annoying. Just remember it doesn't take a large flock of honkers too long to clean up the available feed.

Morning and evening the geese will fly to the same grainfields to feed until something interrupts the flight. Most often that will be a clever hunter who has watched them just long enough to see which way they go. The *next* time they go, he's waiting conveniently along the flyway or right on the feeding site with a spread of decoys and several loads of chilled two's. Any gunner can do the same after a little reconnaissance.

The matter of decoys for these grainfield geese is a small problem, really. Silhouettes cut from plywood, the more the better, do the job as well as full-bodied decoys which are more expensive. Cutting them out of scrap material is a routine job for a home-workshop fan.

Concealment is important in waiting out geese. But it's no problem. The same burlap outfit described before works fine. So will covering up carefully with cornstalks if your vigil happens to take place in a field of harvested corn. You're making like an infantryman, so why not carry one of those small infantry shovels and dig in. It will make your concealment all the harder to detect by decoying geese.

At sunrise one raw morning a few years ago, my friend Lon Parker enjoyed a strange brand of duck shooting he never knew before. He bagged a limit of mallards in a pond he had built himself only half an hour before. Then he rolled up the pond and went home for breakfast. I thought it was a practical joke when he told me about it later. But several days afterward he showed me exactly how it worked.

Every autumn the long trip south is one continuous obstacle course for North American ducks and geese. And nowadays ducks have it tougher than ever. Waterfowlers like Lon Parker have added new obstacles in the form of counterfeit ponds and puddles. Parker found that he could build a duck pond in any bottom-land grainfield and shortly thereafter might have some shooting for mallards or black ducks.

Probably the pioneer in building these counterfeit ponds was one Harold Hann, a veteran Kansas City sportsman, who built his ponds with commercial polyethylene sheeting. He selected a cornfield where ducks were accustomed to feed, spread the sheeting, which is available at any building-supply store, and pegged it down around the edges to keep it from blowing away. Then he placed a good spread of decoys on the "water" and sat down to wait, either in a shallow pit blind or just underneath the "water."

From the air the polyethylene glitters like the water in a wintry marsh on a windy day. I've flown overhead to see for myself. A fresh wind is actually helpful, too, because it ripples the sheeting realistically enough to tempt ducks at least in to good gunning range. Occasionally they drop down all the way and seem surprised only when they discover that the water isn't wet.

Recently the plastic-pond idea has spread to the prairie country of Iowa and Nebraska and even to the fringes of the Great Lakes. Rolled up or folded, enough polyethylene sheeting for a pond is light enough to be carried under the arm, on a sled, or lashed to a pack board. A station wagon can haul a forty- or fifty-foot simulated lake. A pickup truck will do the same job.

Almost every year in many northern states, the duck hunting ends before the legal closing of the season. It can happen when all open water, especially on the smaller ponds and marshes, finally freezes solid. After that, most ducks in any locality move farther south or they congregate far out on the open water of larger lakes, and then commute daily to inland feeding grounds, usually in grainfields. An Ohio sportsman, Tom Henderson, figured out a way to prolong his own shooting until the season is closed officially. His discovery may be suitable to duck-hunting situations elsewhere.

Henderson creates a counterfeit opening on river ice or on a farm pond. It's as elementary as dissolving several boxes of blue Tintex dye or several bottles of blueing in buckets of warm water. These he pours on the ice and the result is a completely genuine-looking, blue patch of "open" water on a pond. After he places decoys all around, he has a spread which very few ducks can pass up when the rest of the landscape is frozen tight.

Henderson has found that it isn't even necessary to build a blind out on the ice. Instead he simply covers himself and huddles nearby on the sled (painted white) he uses to carry decoys and a thermos of hot coffee.

The true test for Henderson's Tintex pond came on the last day of the season. At that late date every duck in the Midwest should have been an expert in detecting counterfeits. Still, Henderson quickly bagged his four birds, which was the limit, and then sat in amazement as waterfowl continued to drop in to his pond all morning long. He only wishes he could patent his phony pond-on-the-ice.

Chapter 10

WATERFOWL DOGS

During a hunting season several years ago the U. S. Fish and Wildlife Service made an intensive study to determine the total shooting kill of waterfowl. What they found is worth considerable examination.

The season's toll amounted to about fifteen million ducks and almost a million geese, or a total of around sixteen million birds. These figures include both retrieved and non-retrieved birds. The non-retrieved portion amounted to over three million birds—21 per cent of the total kill, lost in marshes, sloughs, and waterways across America.

Everywhere during the last ten years there has been increasing emphasis on waterfowl management. As a result, federal, state and even private agencies are collecting data on how many birds are bagged and how many birds are lost. It now appears that over the years our national average for waterfowl loss by crippling is 25 per cent or more. That is a disgraceful waste, to say the least.

This annual loss cuts drastically into our breeding stock of waterfowl as well as into the number of birds we can safely shoot each fall. It's poor business and poor sportsmanship to allow a fourth of our total waterfowl kill to go down a rat hole because of carelessness.

It should be emphasized that the 25 per cent figure for our waterfowl loss was not picked out of the air. It was determined only after long and serious observation by waterfowl experts, by X-raying thousands of dead, crippled and live-trapped ducks. It was even discovered, for example, that about 35 per cent of seventeen hundred birds live-trapped and X-rayed in Illinois were

carrying shot in their bodies. These birds may linger and die long after the season closes. And there is indication that the loss from crippling may be considerably higher than the 25 per cent.

There are a number of reasons for this terrible waste in waterfowl. One reason is trigger-happy shooting, a matter which has been discussed elsewhere. Another reason is the inability to judge distance or range of ducks. Poor marksmanship is a third factor. But just as important as any of these is the failure to retrieve crippled birds.

Some birds, it is sad to report, are not retrieved because the shooters are too lazy to exert themselves and to wade through the deep muck of an average marsh. Others retrieve only those birds which are most desirable to eat, and leave the rest on the water. There is absolutely no excuse for this kind of waste and the culprits should be dealt with severely when caught. But by far the greatest number of birds are not retrieved for lack of a good retrieving dog.

It is almost impossible to overestimate or overemphasize the value of a good dog in any kind of waterfowling. A dog is a pleasure to watch, a companion and a very valuable ally. Some of the greatest moments I can remember in thirty years of waterfowling are some of the "impossible" retrieves made by duck dogs I've known.

Many, many breeds have been used to retrieve waterfowl, but only a few of them are totally qualified to do this job. Since virtually all retrieving must be done from water, which is usually icy or extremely cold, dogs must be especially adapted by their very construction to this unpleasant work. An average house dog might

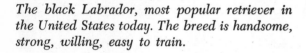

The black Labrador, most popular retriever in the United States today. The breed is handsome, strong, willing, easy to train.

not even be able to survive a long day in a boat or blind under typical duck-hunting conditions. But a good retriever can plunge into icy water time and again and really seem to enjoy the work.

The breeds of dogs most frequently used to retrieve wildfowl today are the Chesapeake, the American water spaniel, the Labrador, the Irish water spaniel, the golden retriever, the springer spaniel, the flat-coated retriever and the curly-coated retriever. One or two other breeds, such as the Newfoundland and the German shorthair pointer, might possibly qualify.

Far and away the most popular retriever in North America today is the Labrador. These handsome animals have good noses, are strong, are adapted to general work with a gun, are superior in the water, and are very hardy and persevering in retrieving any waterfowl. The Labrador's coat is close, short and dense. Beneath the coat the animal is compactly constructed in reality as well as in appearance. An individual given good conditioning possesses tremendous strength

both for hunting on land and for swimming long distances.

It is interesting to note that the Labrador didn't come from Labrador at all, but rather from Newfoundland by way of England. Today there are two classes of Labradors, black and yellow, but there are no structural differences between the two of them.

Besides its excellence as a water dog, the Labrador's great popularity can be attributed to several other reasons. First, it is exceptionally willing and eager to please. Second, most Labradors are friendly and can become good family dogs as well as waterfowl dogs. Third, they are splendid dogs for hunting such upland game as pheasants, rabbits and partridges.

The Chesapeake Bay retriever, which may weigh anywhere from fifty to seventy-five or eighty pounds, is a powerful dog able to cope with virtually any condition of water or elements. Until the past twenty years or so, he was easily the most popular of all American retrievers. The dog's coarse double coat is a tawny brown, or

Yellow Labrador retrieving a mallard and a goose. This fine dog is owned by Joe Linduska of Remington Arms.

rather the color of dead reeds and grasses in autumn. This blends neatly with the average duck blind and helps hide the dog from sharp waterfowl eyes.

It is believed that the first Chesapeakes came to the United States by accident in about 1805 when they were rescued from a sinking ship. On this ship were two puppies, brown in color, named Sailor and Canton. Their progeny became the Chesapeake dogs we know today, although it has taken at least a hundred years to develop them to their precise modern form.

Chesapeakes have been known to swim uninterrupted for as long as thirty minutes in near freezing water in pursuit of crippled ducks. Even after this ordeal the dog suffered no ill effects and would return to the water on command. Perhaps the main reason the Chesapeake is no longer the most popular waterfowl retriever is that a few individuals have developed surly dispositions and are not always easy to train. At least, that is the impression many gunners now have.

Only two breeds of dogs are recognized as being of American origin, and one of these is the handsome American water spaniel. Long familiar to sportsmen, he has not been too popular in recent years for reasons hard to explain. The dog swims naturally and with considerable stamina. He is medium in size, rather short in the legs, sturdy, of typical spaniel character, has a curly coat, and over-all is an active muscular dog. His disposition is very amiable and most water-spaniel owners consider him a dog of the greatest intelligence.

Another breed of growing popularity is the golden retriever. Its origin is uncertain, but it probably comes from a race of Russian sheep dogs which found their way to England more than a century ago by way of a circus. Goldens are strikingly handsome dogs, very powerful, and of good disposition. It is my own experience, at least, that they are not as enthusiastic in the water and in pursuing crippled waterfowl as are the retrievers mentioned before. Of course, there are countless exceptions to this, but I am speaking of the average golden retriever versus the average Labrador or Chesapeake.

The Irish water spaniel is a product of the west coast of Ireland, where hunting waterfowl in the numerous bogs and marshes is an important and unique sport. Perhaps no water dog, unless it would be the Chesapeake, has a coat better adapted for the icy conditions on a typical waterfowling day. The Irish water spaniel is probably a cross between an English water spaniel and the poodle. The topknot, smooth face, very curly hair and great intelligence are probably derived from the poodle. Its general appearance is that of a huge, shaggy, liver-colored dog with a rat-like tail. Most Irish water spaniels are good watchdogs, aloof yet still very companionable with close friends.

The springer spaniel is a good swimmer and can be used to great advantage as a waterfowl retriever. However, it is much better as a flushing and retrieving dog in the uplands, and most springers are used only on rare occasions when upland-hunting masters go duck hunting. A typical springer does not have the strength and stamina to spend long hours in cold water as do the other larger retrievers which are used almost exclusively for waterfowl.

Neither the curly-coated nor the flat-coated retriever is very well known or very popular in the United States today. Not too many sportsmen even know too much about them. However, they are highly capable dogs and make highly valuable companions on any duck-hunting expedition.

It is a rare retriever of good breeding which does not take naturally to its work. In other words, teaching a retriever to retrieve is seldom a difficult task. On the other hand, training is a very pleasant pastime and can furnish a duck hunter many pleasant hours of recreation during the off season.

A most important point in retriever training is basic instruction in obedience. An obstreperous or undisciplined dog cannot be tolerated in a boat or blind. A retriever should be taught to lie down and to stay down quietly when he is commanded to do so. He must never become restless or a nuisance. It is also necessary that a retriever respond to the command "heel." When

Golden retriever, a big dog and good swimmer growing in popularity.

jump-shooting or sneaking up on ponds on hands and knees, the dog should hunker down and follow just behind or just beside the hunter. In any other case, he will flush the ducks long before a hunter can reach close enough shooting range.

There is an alternative to teaching a dog yourself and that is to employ a professional trainer. But the most important thing, whether the dog is trained at home or by a professional, is to give him plenty of exercise and experience. Dogs can be trained by retrieving live pigeons all year long. There is no closed season on this activity.

There are many good volumes about retriever training on bookshelves nowadays, and it is a very good idea to obtain one of these while your retriever is still a puppy. Another good idea is to consult with other sportsmen who have already successfully trained retrievers for the field. Still another bit of good advice is to join one of the retriever clubs that now exist in almost every community across the country.

No retriever is any better than its physical condition. A poorly conditioned dog cannot swim the long distances that are often necessary. Besides physical conditioning before opening day, a dog's diet becomes an extremely important factor. Correct feeding is particularly important among such large breeds as retrievers. And that is doubly true during their growing-up period. Most of these dogs weigh only a pound or two at birth, but in another year they grow to about eighty to ninety pounds or more. A human being requires ten to twelve times that long to reach the same growth.

Because retrievers do grow so fast, attention should be given to proper diet. A young retriever's diet should be fortified with calcium and phosphorous, vitamin D and proteins. It is true that feeding a large dog can be very expensive, but if you are forced to cut corners, wait until the dog reaches maturity.

Many retriever owners are constantly in doubt about how much to feed their dogs. There is no correct answer to cover all situations. Most commercial dog foods are the result of much research

Retriever must be willing to plunge over and over into icy water as this Lab, Blackie, is doing. Crippled duck is just out of the picture.

and they provide fairly complete and well-balanced diets. For commercial foods, here are a few rules of thumb that can be used as a basis in feeding an active retriever. For young growing retrievers, figure about one ounce of wet meal or canned food per pound of body weight of the dog per day. For older animals figure one half to three fourths of an ounce per pound of body weight for the dog each day.

If you prefer dry meal, figure one to two pounds of dry meal per day per thirty-five pounds of dog. All these figures may be increased slightly during those busy periods in autumn when the dogs are frequently working in the field. During other periods, when the dogs are largely idle, the rations can be cut slightly.

Of course, your dog should be immunized against distemper, rabies and any other diseases locally common among dogs.

Lab at work, swimming after dead duck in Lake Erie.

Chapter 11

THE DUCK HUNTER'S EQUIPMENT

As we have pointed out often before, and as any experienced waterfowler knows, duck and goose hunting can be cold businesses. Waterfowling isn't really an active sport unless you are jump-shooting, and so it calls for very warm clothing. A good part of duck hunting means sitting in a blind, and the new insulated underwear and insulated clothing are excellent for this. But for walking long distances and slogging through marshes, they can quickly become too warm.

The ideal outfit for hunting on a very cold day in a blind is a set of insulated underwear over which woolen pants and shirt are worn. I also like to wear a soft woolen dickey or turtle-neck sweater under my shirt. On the coldest days a quilted down jacket is ideal. On other days a standard canvas or duck-hunting jacket is fine, and the older and more weathered it is the better. For headgear the fur-lined hats with ear muffs that can be tied on top of the hat or lowered over the ears are just about perfect.

Of course, waterfowling may also be done in warmer climates and on bluebird days. In these situations a hunter will simply have to follow his own preference to meet local conditions. But if he is wise, he will always be prepared for the worst, because among other things, autumn weather is extremely changeable and uncertain.

It may seem like gilding the lily but many waterfowlers wear drab camouflage-type suits over their regular heavy clothing. Sometimes this camouflaged material can also double as foul-weather gear, which every duck hunter should also have available in case of rain or snow. The alternative to the camouflaged clothing is to tint or otherwise paint camouflaged designs on old outer garments. The paint and colors used should match as nearly as possible the color of dead fall vegetation in the marshes.

Most duck hunters believe that the vision of a duck is very sensitive to such bright colors as red, orange and yellow. Maybe this is true, and just on the slight possibility that it is, hunters should probably avoid wearing such bright hues. However, I really believe that ducks are far more likely to notice movement or motion of a hunter in the blind than the color of his clothing. Bright objects (such as eyeglasses) also make ducks shy away.

During a long vigil in a cold blind there is nothing more welcome at intervals than a hot beverage and perhaps a hot snack. If a warm clubhouse is nearby, this isn't so important. But if no clubhouse exists or if it is far away, it is a good idea to carry a vacuum container of scalding-hot coffee or tea or hot chocolate. Keep in mind that of the three, hot chocolate gives quick energy faster and in greater volume than coffee or tea. Many hunters like to carry along a can or two of soup and a small stove to cook it on while waiting in the blind.

Most duck hunting requires either hip boots or waders. Which of these the hunter obtains de-

Hip boots or waders are essential in nearly all kinds of waterfowling. Insulated boots have value because water is always cold.

Often a boat must be used as a blind—and an outboard is invaluable for reaching remote areas of marshland. But bright-colored motors must be covered up—as here. (JOHNSON MOTORS PHOTO)

pends more or less upon the situations he will face. Sometimes I have suffered discomfort all through a day because cold water came over the top of my hip boots while I was retrieving a bird or putting out decoys. On the other hand, I have labored unnecessarily across soggy cornfields while wearing waders that I didn't need. It's a

Handy canvas bag used for carrying decoys to the shooting area. Decoys are bulky and not easy to carry in quantity through boggy places.

Duck call with rubber bellows to imitate feeding chuckle of puddle ducks.

Hunter tries calling ducks. A good call in hands of an expert can be a great help.

matter of taste, preference and need. However, it's a good idea to consider the new insulated models no matter which type of gear is selected.

Waterfowlers are not as gadget conscious or as gadget happy as some other outdoorsmen. But there are several items of equipment that can make any hunt a bit more pleasant. A good example of this would be the small tent or camp heater, which is just as good when placed inside a blind. Hunters nowadays can use alcohol as fuel in these heaters because it does not give off toxic fumes inside an enclosed area. Handwarmers are handy to stuff inside pockets and it's a good idea to carry along a small cushion to sit on inside the blind. Lip ice is helpful to prevent chapping, and glycerin is good dressing for the hands. I also carry along two or three pairs of gloves, which can be changed off as one or more pairs get wet during the course of hunting.

Many duck-hunting situations require boats or some kind of craft to transport the hunter out to his blind or to his shooting area. The type of boat very commonly in use, especially in the eastern half of the United States, is the double-ended wooden punt boat. These old punt boats are more traditional than they are useful. They were designed in the days before aluminum and they are both unwieldy and hard for anyone but a very experienced punter to maneuver, especially

Small plastic dinghies like this can have some use in pond and pothole shooting.

Handy guide's rig for taking shallow-draft duck boat to water's edge. This is handy for the freelancing duck hunter.

in the dark when most duck-hunting days begin.

Many veteran duck hunters will not agree with this but I believe the most versatile, dependable and durable duck boat for most situations is the very shallow draft, light aluminum johnboat. This can be rowed, pulled, punted, or paddled wherever there is enough water to float it—and it doesn't need very much water. Of course, it should be painted a dull brown or olive because the natural aluminum finish can cause ducks to spook.

Every waterfowler eventually acquires a number of duck and goose calls. If he learns how to use them properly, they can increase his pleasure and maybe even increase his bag. But the hunter who is not proficient with a call would do far better to leave it at home. Poor callers can frighten away more ducks than they attract. More times than not a hunter is far better off

just retreating deeper into his blind and depending upon his decoys to lure the ducks.

Most duck calls on the market are intended for mallards. Because effective calling varies greatly from region to region, a call which is effective in the northern Midwest may not be nearly as good in the south. It's a matter of trial and error until a hunter finds a call which will work for him and one on which he can become very proficient.

In much of the Mississippi flyway most hunters use what is called a highball. This is nothing more than a very loud series of quacks designed to pull high-flying ducks down in to range. The fact that it is still in wide use is evidence that it often works. Elsewhere a coarse guttural feeding sound will attract far more ducks, especially early and late in the day when many ducks are actively looking for feeding areas.

A session with a hand trap and plenty of clay pigeons is great practice before and during the waterfowl season.

But maybe the greatest skill of all is knowing when to call and when not to call. Keep calling only when ducks seem to lose interest and to swing far away from you. When they head toward you, be quiet. A basic rule of duck hunting is that as long as ducks are coming your way do not move, do not call and do not shoot.

There are three good ways to learn successful duck calling: from expert callers, from records and from ducks. The feeding sounds can be learned by listening to ducks feeding in local parks or zoos or even in nearby refuges. A very successful hunter I know has spent many long hours making tape recordings of feeding ducks. During spare time before the waterfowling season he can go over these again and again at

Showing value of short barrel on double gun for jump-shooting. Hunter can swing faster to get on target.

home, all the while perfecting his technique. A certain amount of skill in duck calling can also be attained with the duck-call records now available in sporting-goods stores.

Calling geese is similar to calling ducks in that you are better off not to try it until you have become proficient. A very good goose caller can seemingly talk to geese and coax them down in to range. On the other hand, I have seen geese veer sharply away at the first call given by an inexperienced caller. A beginner might find help in the several goose-calling records now available.

What kind of gun is best for waterfowling? That question is nearly impossible to answer because waterfowling contains so many variables. One good bit of advice is to use the scatter-gun with which you as an individual can shoot best. The best gauge, choke and load of a duck gun depends on the kind of shooting required of it. For pass shooting and long-range shooting, as well as for all goose hunting, a full-bored gun which throws heavy shot in dense patterns is needed. For much of the shooting over decoys, when ducks work in very closely, lighter gauges, finer shot and more-open barrels might be satisfactory.

Shallow draft boats like these have great potential in many duck hunting situations. They're small enough to be carried cartop from place to place.

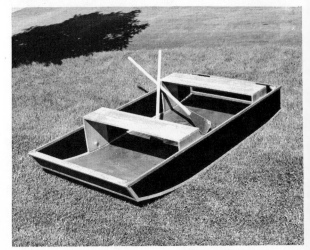

Highly valuable item for finding way to blind and placing out decoys in predawn is a waterproof, nonsinkable flashlight like this one—called Dynalite.

A white bed sheet is used as camouflage during winter snow shooting.

Several years ago, on an Indiana public hunting area, 2595 shotguns (used by hunters) were examined and the results would probably indicate that America's favorite duck gun is undoubtedly the twelve-gauge pump gun with a full choke barrel. Of the guns censused, 25 per cent were twelve-gauge automatics and only 11 per cent were twelve-gauge doubles. Less than 3 per cent were three-inch magnum twelve-gauges, and only a few assorted other gauges were used. The types of chokes used were not completely noted, but most of them were full-bored.

At many of the older duck clubs around the United States it is the law, written or unwritten, that only double-barreled shotguns will be used. While they may be accurate and entirely suitable for waterfowling, waterfowl biologists have pointed out that double-barreled guns are probably not in the best interest of conservation. The third shot in a pump or automatic is extremely valuable in collecting cripples which might otherwise escape. Incidentally, no more than three shells can be carried in any shotgun while hunting ducks or geese in the United States. If the gun has capacity for more than three shots, it must be plugged.

There is considerable evidence that the shell or load is far more important than the shotgun used in hunting waterfowl. In a joint study with Winchester Arms, Frank Bellrose of the Illinois Natural History Survey discovered that an average of five Number 4 pellets is needed to kill a mallard duck. If it is struck with less than five Number 4's, it may become a cripple and odds are that it will never be included in anybody's bag.

With waterfowl populations dwindling, as we have noted elsewhere in this book, it is every sportsman's moral obligation to use a heavy enough load and then not to use it until the birds are absolutely within killing range. I often hear of hunters making spectacular shots at eighty and a hundred yards. But instead of publicizing these incidents, shooting at such ranges should be entirely deplored. There simply is no such thing as a hundred-yard gun and a hundred-yard load. Not even the finest magnum shells manufactured today can give a shooter this kind of range.

Uninformed shooters are often heard to remark that modern magnums double their range and double the killing power at this range. But this simply isn't true. A magnum-shot shell is only a more effective load within normal shooting ranges. It has nothing to do with greater velocity or penetration because a magnum will not shoot harder or farther than a standard load. Instead it offers more pattern density. If a magnum load hits harder, it's because it hits the target more often with more pellets.

In the three-inch, twelve-gauge, magnum-shot shell there are 253 Number 4 pellets in the 1⅞ ounce load. In a standard Winchester Super-X load there are 169 Number 4 pellets. At forty yards the big magnum will deliver an average of ten and a half Number 4 pellets into a duck while the standard Super-X will deliver seven pellets at the same range. The total energy hitting the duck at forty yards is half again as great with the magnum. However, remember that the range is not increased.

Every American might well contemplate the philosophy of Nat Buckingham, one of America's best-known sportsmen and duck hunters. "I never gamble when I shoot waterfowl," he claims. "I believe in taking the bird close and hitting him very, very hard with big shot from a big gun at the closest reasonable range."

Winchester Model 101 over-and-under shotgun.

Winchester Model 1200.

Winchester Model 1400.

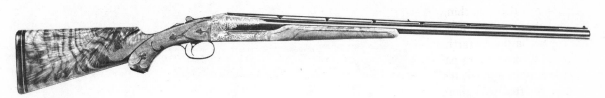

Winchester Model 21 Grand American.

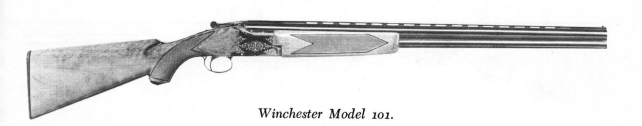

Winchester Model 12 Pigeon.

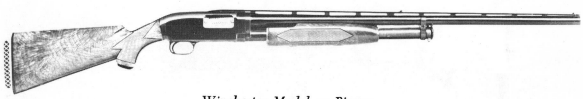

Winchester Model 101.

Winchester Model 59.

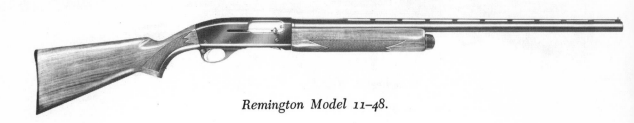

Remington Model 11–48.

Remington Model 870 "Wingmaster."

Remington Model 1100.

Ithaca Model 66 Supersingle.

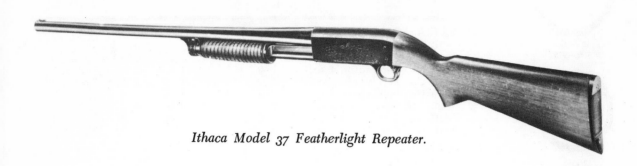

Ithaca Model 37 Featherlight Repeater.

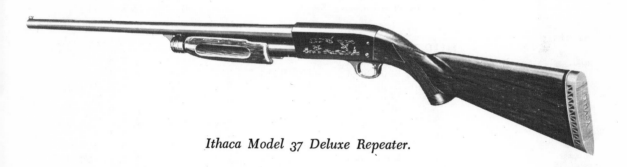

Ithaca Model 37 Deluxe Repeater.

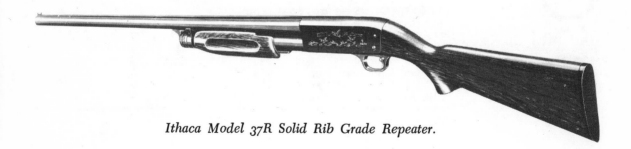

Ithaca Model 37R Solid Rib Grade Repeater.

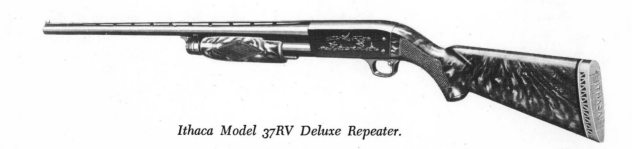

Ithaca Model 37RV Deluxe Repeater.

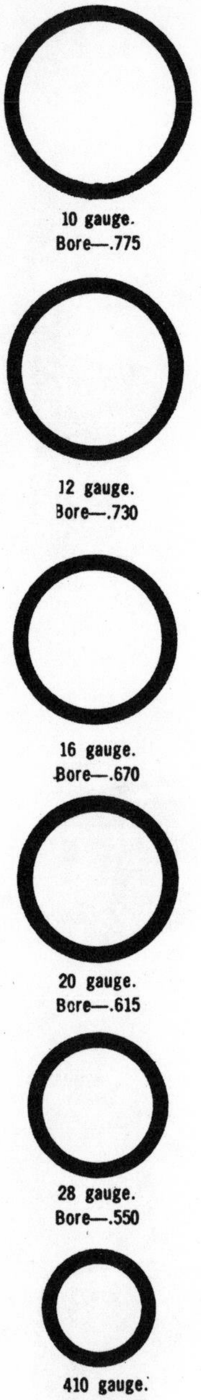

REMINGTON PLASTIC SHOT SHELLS

Gauge and Brand	Length Shell Ins.	Powder Equiv. Drams	Shot Oz.	Size Shot
EXTRA LONG RANGE—Flat-Top Crimp				
10 Ga. Remington Exp.	2⅞	4¾	1⅝	4
12 Ga. Remington Exp.	2¾	3¾	1¼	BB, 2, 4, 5, 6, 7½, 9
16 Ga. Remington Exp.	2¾	3	1⅛	2, 4, 5, 6, 7½, 9
16 Ga. Remington Exp.	2¾	3¼	1⅛	4, 5, 6, 7½
20 Ga. Remington Exp.	2¾	2¾	1	2, 4, 5, 6, 7½, 9
*28 Ga. Remington Exp.	2¾	2¼	¾	4, 6, 7½, 9
*410 Ga. Remington Exp.	2½	......	½	4, 5, 6, 7½, 9
*410 Ga. Remington Exp.	3	....	¾	4, 5, 6, 7½, 9
MAGNUM LOADS				
10 Ga. Remington Exp.	3½	5	2	2, 4
12 Ga. Remington Exp.	2¾	4	1½	2, 4, 5, 6, 7½
12 Ga. Remington Exp.	3	4½	1⅞	BB, 2, 4
12 Ga. Remington Exp.	3	4¼	1⅝	BB, 2, 4, 5, 6
16 Ga. Remington "SP"	2¾	3½	1¼	2, 4, 6
20 Ga. Remington "SP"	2¾	3	1⅛	2, 4, 6, 7½
20 Ga. Remington "SP"	3	3¼	1¼	2, 4, 6, 7½
FIELD LOADS—Flat-Top Crimp				
12 Ga. Shur Shot	2¾	3	1	4, 5, 6, 8
12 Ga. Shur Shot	2¾	3	1⅛	4, 5, 6, 8, 9
12 Ga. Shur Shot	2¾	3¼	1⅛	4, 5, 6, 7½, 8, 9
*12 Ga. Shur Shot	2¾	3¼	1¼	7½, 8
16 Ga. Shur Shot	2¾	3¼	1¼	7½, 8 (Nickel)
16 Ga. Shur Shot	2¾	2¾	1⅛	4, 5, 6, 7½, 8, 9
16 Ga. Shur Shot	2¾	2½	1	4, 5, 6, 8, 9
20 Ga. Shur Shot	2¾	2¼	⅞	4, 5, 6, 8, 9
20 Ga. Shur Shot	2¾	2½	1	4, 5, 6, 7½, 8, 9
SCATTER LOADS—Roll Crimp				
12 Ga. Shur Shot	2¾	3	1⅛	8
16 Ga. Shur Shot	2¾	2½	1	8
20 Ga. Shur Shot	2¾	2¼	⅞	8
TARGET LOADS—Flat-Top Crimp				
*12 Ga. Shur Shot	2¾	3	1⅛	7½, 8, 9
*12 Ga. Shur Shot	2¾	2¾	1⅛	7½, 8, 9
*16 Ga. Shur Shot	2¾	2½	1	9
*20 Ga. Shur Shot	2¾	2¼	⅞	9
*28 Ga. Remington Exp.	2¾	2¼	¾	9
*410 Ga. Remington Exp.	2½	.....	½	9
*410 Ga. Remington Exp.	3		¾	9

*Paper cases

10 gauge.
Bore—.775

12 gauge.
Bore—.730

16 gauge.
Bore—.670

20 gauge.
Bore—.615

28 gauge.
Bore—.550

410 gauge.
Bore—.410

*Shotgun gauges—
actual size.*

Sample catalog listing of shells and comparative shot sizes.

FEDERAL SHOT SHELLS

Load No.	Length Shell ins.	Gauge	Powder Drams Equiv.	Ounces Shot	SHOT SIZES Standard Shot
HI-POWER Brand					
HP127	2¾	12	3¾	1¼	BB, 2, 4, 5, 6, 7½, 9
HP163	2⁹⁄₁₆	16	3	1⅛	2, 4, 5, 6, 7½, 9
HP164	2¾	16	3¼	1⅛	2, 4, 5, 6, 7½
HP203	2¾	20	2¾	1	2, 4, 5, 6, 7½, 9
HP281	2¾	28	2¼	¾	4, 6, 7½
HP412	2½	410	Max	½	4, 5, 6, 7½
HP413	3	410	Max	¾	4, 5, 6, 7½
MAGNUM LOADS					
HP130	2¾	12	4	1½	2, 4, 5, 6
HP131	3	12	4½	1⅞	BB, 2, 4, 5
HP129	3	12	4¼	1⅝	2, 4, 5, 6
HP165	2¾	16	3½	1¼	2, 4, 6
HP205	2¾	20	3	1⅛	2, 4, 6, 7½
HP207	3	20	3¼	1¼	2, 4, 6, 7½
HP282	2¾	28	2¾	1	6, 7½, 8, 9
MONARK Brand					
M120	2¾	12	3	1	4, 5, 6, 8
M121	2¾	12	3	1⅛	4, 5, 6, 8, 9
M123	2¾	12	3¼	1⅛	4, 5, 6, 7½, 8, 9
M124	2¾	12	3¼	1¼	7½, 8
M161	2⁹⁄₁₆	16	2½	1	4, 5, 6, 8, 9
M162	2⁹⁄₁₆	16	2¾	1⅛	4, 5, 6, 7½, 8, 9
M201	2¾	20	2¼	⅞	4, 5, 6, 8, 9
M202	2¾	20	2½	1	4, 5, 6, 7½, 8, 9
OPEN LOADS					
M125	2¾	12	3	1⅛	8
M160	2¾	16	2½	1	8
M200	2¾	20	2¼	⅞	8
TARGET LOADS					
M119	2¾	12	2¾	1⅛	7½, 8, 9
T122	2¾	12	3	1⅛	7½, 8, 9
S166	2¾	16	2½	1	8, 9
S206	2¾	20	2¼	⅞	8, 9
S280	2¾	28	2¼	¾	9
S412	2½	410	Max	½	9
S413	3	410	Max	¾	9

SHOT					COMPARATIVE SIZES									BUCK SHOT					
NO.	DUST	12	11	10	9	8	7½	7	6	5	4	2	AIR RIFLE	BB	4	3	1	0	00	000
DIAMETER IN INCHES	.04	.05	.06	.07	.08	.09	.095	.10	.11	.12	.13	.15	.175	.18	.24	.25	.30	.32	.33	.36
APPROX. PELLETS IN 1 OZ.	4565	2385	1380	870	585	410	350	290	225	170	135	90	55	50	340 lb.	300 lb.	175 lb.	145 lb.	130 lb.	98 lb.

Chapter 12

WILDFOWL COOKERY

Not the least of the dividends of a typical duck hunt is the delicious duck dinner which follows. Many species of waterfowl must rank with the finest of wild meats and virtually all of them are good eating if properly prepared. But first there is the matter of plucking and dressing before they are ready for the table.

First let's state that the sooner it is done the easier it is to pluck any duck or goose. Plucking a duck immediately after it is shot is not so difficult, but often this isn't convenient to do. In addition, some sportsmen believe that a duck should be hung for several days before it is plucked. I do not happen to agree with this theory and believe that ducks should be plucked and dressed no later than the same day they are shot. This is doubly true if any shot has penetrated the intestine or the gall of the duck.

The simplest but not necessarily the easiest way of plucking is to use a thumb and forefinger, picking clumps of feathers and moving against the grain. In other words, from tail to head of the duck. Some shooters first remove the head and tail before they start plucking, but this is a matter of personal preference. I prefer to leave the feet on the bird because it gives me a good handle for the hand not used in plucking. If the duck has been dead some time and if water and heat are available, dipping the duck briefly into a bucket of boiling water will be of some slight help in removing the feathers.

A far more convenient method is to bring a pan of water almost to the boiling point, then drop several sticks of paraffin, the same type used in canning jelly and jams, into the boiling water and allow it to melt and form a melted

wax on top of the hot water. Five or six standard cakes of paraffin will be enough to dress all of the ducks you are likely to bag in one season.

After the paraffin has melted, dip the duck into the bucket until it is entirely covered with a thin coating of wax. Remove, allow the carcass to drain thoroughly, and place the duck aside for a few minutes until the wax stiffens and completely congeals. After the paraffin has congealed and cooled, it can be peeled off the duck in virtually the same manner as peeling a tangerine. All but the tiniest of pinfeathers are removed in the process. Pop the pieces of wax and feathers back into the bucket because they can be used over and over again all season long.

A few waterfowlers dip their ducks into a bucket of water to which heaping tablespoons of detergent have been added. This is said to be a superior method for plucking. Perhaps so, but I am not sure that I would like to have the suds on my meat.

After the duck is plucked, you can remove the head and feet. With a sharp knife make a V-shaped incision just under the breast and toward the vent. Do not cut too deeply or you will puncture the intestine. After you have made this cut, you can reach inside and easily pull out all of the entrails. It may be necessary to reach inside the cavity with your knife to cut free the trachea and the gullet, which are attached to the body of the duck. Not all duck hunters believe in washing the duck either inside or out after it has been dressed and drawn. However, I think there is no harm in doing this.

If the ducks are to be frozen rather than cooked immediately, it's much better to seal individual ducks in the plastic freezer bags which are available nowadays. If they are not sealed up in this manner, ducks tend to become dehydrated after not too long a time.

Still another good and easy way to dress any kind of waterfowl is simply to skin back the breast portion of the duck rather than to pluck the duck, and then with a very sharp knife carefully fillet out the two pieces of breast meat. Especially on the diving ducks, virtually no other good meat remains and the rest of the bird can be discarded. On some of the large puddle ducks such as the mallards and blacks, the rest of the carcass can be skinned and the meat thereon used in pressed duck and in making stews. Filleting is a very simple task; it takes only a bit of practice to become an expert, almost in the same manner as practice can make anyone an expert at filleting fish.

Any strong taste that exists in ducks, and this has been greatly exaggerated, usually exists in the fat the ducks accumulate under the skin. When dressing a duck, no matter whether you use the entire carcass or only the fillets, it is a good idea to trim off all excess fat.

All ducks, and especially geese, can be tenderized by hanging them for two or three days before cooking. They should be completely dressed before this hanging and they should be placed where the temperature hovers between thirty-five and forty degrees. At these temperatures, ducks will keep for as long as three or four or even five days, depending upon how quickly they have been dressed after shooting.

No two sportsmen and no two cooks agree on exactly how ducks should be handled. One school believes that wild duck should be eaten nearly rare and another school believes that they should be cooked until they are as tough and dry as leather. Probably the best method lies somewhere in between, and herewith follow some of the most delicious and exciting recipes for cooking duck which I have been able to accumulate in many years.

Pressed Mallard. My friend Frank Sayers enjoys cooking ducks as much as he enjoys hunting them. Several times every season he makes a huge production of preparing his special pressed mallard. All waterfowlers who have never been able to taste this elegant yet robust concoction are most unfortunate. Frank roasts four mallards in a 400-degree oven for about twelve minutes, then places them on a wooden carving board. Very neatly he removes the breasts, or rather fillets them, and then sets the rest of the carcasses aside. The carcasses are then placed in a duck press and the liquors and juices are extracted.

Beforehand two sauces have been prepared in chafing dishes. The first chafing dish contains melted butter blended with currant jelly. To this add a teaspoon of salt, a pinch of cayenne pepper, a tablespoon of Worcestershire sauce, a few drops of Tabasco, and the liquid squeezed from the duck carcass. Now the breasts of the duck are floated in the chafing dish that contains this sauce.

A second sauce is made by grinding up the duck hearts and livers after they have been sautéed and salt and pepper have been added. The ground-up hearts and livers are then mixed with a minced heart of celery, diced onions, and enough dry sherry to make a thick liquid. After the breasts are simmered slowly and thoroughly in the first sauce, they are covered with the second sauce and served. Most people who have tasted Frank's pressed duck say it is too good to be true.

Kelsor Smith's Recipe. During every hunting season Kelsor Smith, the busy chef at Remington Farms near Chestertown, Maryland, cooks many hundreds of ducks. He also receives as many requests for his mouth-watering recipe for preparing mallards, pintails or blacks. Here's how it goes.

Place the ducks, any number of them, in a pan breast up. Sprinkle each duck with one tablespoon of cooking sherry. Season each duck with one-half teaspoon of celery salt, one-half teaspoon of onion salt, one-half teaspoon of celery seed, one-quarter teaspoon of curry, one teaspoon of salt, one-quarter teaspoon of pepper. Let the ducks sit in the pan from one-half to a full hour.

Now chop one small onion and one stalk of celery and place it in the pan, add a quarter inch to a half inch of water, and bake at 500 degrees until the breasts are brown—this takes about twenty minutes. Turn the ducks over and bake until the backs are brown. Now cover and cook one more hour at 300 degrees. The total cooking time is two hours. If dressing is desired, use any poultry recipe inside the duck.

Lew Baker's Recipe. Several years ago my hunting friend Lew Baker prepared a brace of canvasbacks and the result was as memorable as the hunting trip on which we bagged the ducks. After carefully cleaning and hanging the canvasbacks for two days, Lew stuffed each one with a quartered onion and a slice of lemon, then filled the cavity with heavily peppered sauerkraut and slices of apple in about equal quantities. After sewing up the birds, Lew rubbed them with flour, salt and pepper before placing them in a roasting pan.

Next Lew packed sauerkraut tightly around the birds and added plenty of sauerkraut juice in the bottom of the pan. He sprinkled a tablespoon apiece of granulated sugar on the tops of the birds and then roasted them until brown and very tender. The ducks and sauerkraut were served with coleslaw and cold bottles of ale. If you do not believe that this was an extraordinary dinner, just try it sometime.

Broiled or Fried Fillets. Just about the simplest and surely one of the most delicious ways to cook any duck is to broil the fillets over charcoal or to deep-fry them in peanut oil. They can be cooked either rare, medium or well done to suit anybody's taste. When broiling the ducks, I usually make a liquor of vinegar, melted butter and seasoning with which to baste the fillets during cooking.

Duck Stroganoff. There is something about wild ducks which inspires many outdoor cooks to elaborate recipes. A good example is this one which can be called duck Stroganoff. The ingredients are: three or four ducks from which the meat has been cut into bite-size chunks, salt, pepper, paprika, nutmeg, butter or cooking oil, two medium onions chopped fine, one cup of sour cream, two tablespoons of tomato sauce, and a half pound of mushrooms either fresh or canned.

After browning the onions in butter, place the duck pieces in the pan to brown, then remove the meat and keep it hot. Brown the mushrooms in the duck juices and return the meat to the skillet, then season it with salt, pepper, paprika, and a liberal sprinkling of the nutmeg. Add tomato sauce, more butter or cooking oil if needed, and simmer the whole works for about an hour and a half or until the meat is very tender. Add small amounts of hot water to keep the juices at about a constant level. At the end add half the sour cream and stir. Cook for another ten or fifteen minutes over a *very* low heat, stir in the remainder of the sour cream and serve immediately over wild rice.

Roast Duck Supreme. The chef's specialty at a large duck-shooting club on western Lake Erie, which is called roast duck supreme, is prepared as follows. Soak any number of large ducks in salt water over night. After this, salt, pepper and use celery salt inside the ducks. Place quartered apples, onions and celery leaves inside the ducks, then cover them with bacon or salt-pork slices and place them in a roaster. Cook the ducks breast side up in two inches of consommé or water in a closed roaster in a 350-degree oven for three and a half hours, basting frequently. To pass the time away while the ducks are cooking, the chef can prepare the following orange sauce, which some shooters prefer although others do not.

Ingredients for the orange sauce are: a quarter cup of butter, a half teaspoon of salt, one and a half cups of consommé, two tablespoons of currant jelly, a dash of cayenne pepper, the grated rind of one orange, three-quarters cup of orange juice, fresh if possible, one jigger of dry sherry wine and a tablespoon of flour. The butter is melted in a double boiler, and the flour, salt and cayenne pepper are blended in gradually. Next the consommé is added; then orange rind, jelly and sherry are blended in. The oven is turned up to 400 degrees to brown the ducks, which are brushed with some of the orange juice. They are cooked fifteen minutes more before serving, and the remaining orange sauce is served on the side.

Crisped Teal. Shooters in search of a delicious recipe for teal or wood ducks might try this one, which is called crisped teal. It requires very little preparation, very little effort and few ingredients. The small ducks are cut or split in half, then they are roasted with the outside of the ducks up for about thirty minutes in a 450-degree oven. Just before removing them from the oven, they can be brushed with melted butter in which a clove or two of garlic has been crushed. When the skin is crisp, the ducks are ready to eat.

Barbecued Coot and Peppered Coot. Many shooters consider coot highly inedible, but this isn't necessarily true, and herewith I submit two recipes for coot which are well worth any outdoor cook's time and effort. The first is called barbecued coot.

Take any number of coot and cut the breasts, wings and legs into bite-size pieces. Marinate these for about two hours—not longer—in a liquor of sauterne or dry sherry. Now skewer the pieces alternately with carrots, onions or other vegetables and bacon. Broil these over coals of charcoal, basting frequently with the same marinade liquor.

This next coot recipe, called peppered coot, calls for four birds dressed, skinned, cleaned and cut for frying. It also requires a half teaspoon of sage, a half teaspoon of freshly ground pepper, one-half cup of flour, two tablespoons of dried or chopped parsley, one large green pepper chopped up, one garlic bud finely chopped, one medium-size onion chopped, and one teaspoon Worcestershire sauce. Cut the meat from the breast and leg bones, removing any fat. Salt to taste. Brown the meat in a Dutch oven in a mixture of bacon fat and butter, after dredging in a mixture of flour, sage, and freshly ground pepper. Fry separately in butter all the ingredients and pour over the meat. Cover and simmer for about two hours, adding water if necessary. The finished product is enough to make any shooter change his mind about coot.

Wild Duck Chinese Style. Tracy Balcomb, president of the George Weidemann Brewing Company, in Newport, Kentucky, offers this delicious recipe for cooking wild duck Chinese style. Naturally, one of the ingredients is beer.

The recipe calls for two two-pound wild ducks of any kind, two cloves of minced garlic, one tablespoon of salt, one-half teaspoon of freshly ground pepper, one-quarter cup of melted butter, one apple halved, one-quarter cup of dry mustard, one-half cup of beer, two tablespoons of soy sauce, one cup of apricot preserves, and one tablespoon of lemon juice. Mix to a paste the garlic, salt, and pepper, rub it into the ducks, and brush the breasts heavily with butter. Place a half apple in each duck, and arrange the ducks in a shallow roasting pan breast up. Roast in a 400-degree oven for fifteen minutes.

Next mix together the mustard, beer, soy sauce, apricot preserves and lemon juice. Reduce the heat in the oven to 350 degrees, pour the sauce over the duck, and roast thirty minutes longer, basting frequently. It serves four people normally, but is just about right for two duck hunters who are hungry enough to eat the camp chef raw.

Wild Goose. Wild goose has a reputation for being tough and stringy and often the reputation is deserved. However, the meat of young geese, particularly, is delicious, nutritious, juicy and when properly prepared extremely good.

Early in the year many wild geese are very fat and this can be a problem in cooking. However, there is a simple recipe which takes this fat into consideration and which requires very little effort on the part of the cook. It goes as follows. Stuff any large goose with any good dressing you like and put it in a 450-degree oven in an open roaster for not over thirty minutes with the breast down. After this period, take the roaster out of the oven and pour off all the fat that has been rendered out. With the oven reset at 350 degrees, replace the goose in the roaster —this time with the breast up—and cover it with a clean white cotton cloth. Cook until it is done, or about thirty minutes per pound of bird.

Thanksgiving Goose. Years ago it was customary in my family, as in many German families, to cook a goose for Thanksgiving. Here is how my mother did it. The necessary ingredients include: a large honker, snow or blue goose, a quarter cup of butter, a half cup of uncooked rice, three sticks of celery, one medium-size onion, two cups of water, one and a half cups of ground cranberries, two chicken bouillon cubes, one sprig of parsley, one teaspoon of salt, one teaspoon of freshly ground pepper. Stuffing is made by melting butter in a skillet, adding rice, onion and celery, and then cooking slowly while stirring constantly. When the rice is slightly brown and the cranberries and all the rest of ingredients have been added, cover and cook slowly until the rice is tender. If the rice had a tendency to stick, add water. The stuffing is allowed to cool while the oven warms up to about 350 degrees. As soon as the stuffing is cool enough to handle, place it inside the goose, and put the goose in a roaster breast up. Basting it in its own juices, cook it for about four hours for a six- to ten-pound bird.

Other Goose Recipes

Another good way to cook a small goose is to use the recipe described before for ducks with sauerkraut. The meat of a wild goose can also be used in the duck Stroganoff recipe given before. Equally delicious is the filleted breast of a wild goose broiled over hickory charcoal. It may be necessary to cut the fillets from larger geese into thin strips before broiling. Use a liquor of vinegar, melted butter, and seasonings to baste the goose while it is being broiled.

Duck with Mushroom Gravy. One final water-fowl recipe that we have tried and enjoyed is one called duck with mushroom gravy suggested by Joe Bates, author of *The Outdoor Cook's Bible.* For this two ducks are needed, plus one sliced onion, a half cup of butter or margarine, salt and pepper, one bay leaf, two cups of water, one cup of fresh sliced mushrooms, two table-spoons of flour, and one-eighth teaspoon of thyme. The ducks are disjointed into serving-size pieces. Brown the meat and the onion in fat until the onion is transparent and the duck a golden brown. Pour off the drippings into an-other skillet, season with salt and pepper, and add the water and bay leaf. Cover and cook over moderate heat for an hour and a half.

In a second skillet containing the drippings, sauté the sliced mushrooms and stir in the flour and thyme until the mixture is smooth. Add this to the ducks and continue to cook them slowly for about thirty minutes longer. Use one-half cup of wine instead of water, if desired. If you lack the mushrooms, omit the flour and substitute a can of mushroom soup. Serve with rice or barley.

Wild-Rice Casserole. To serve wild rice with wild duck is almost traditional in places, and here is a particularly elegant wild-rice casserole as prepared by Isabel Sayers. The ingredients include: one pound of wild rice (cooked and drained), one pound of mild sausage, one pound of fresh mushrooms, one cup of onions chopped, one-half cup of toasted sliced almonds, one-fourth cup of flour, one-half cup of milk, two and one-half cups of chicken bouillon, one table-spoon salt, one-half teaspoon pepper, a pinch of oregano, thyme and marjoram, and an optional Tabasco-dash or two. Sauté the sausage and drain enough fat from sausage to sauté onions and mushrooms. Make a sauce of flour and milk, and add chicken bouillon. Simmer until thick. Add seasoning and other ingredients, pour in casserole and top with almonds. Bake for thirty minutes in a 350-degree oven.

Chapter 13

THE FUTURE OF WATERFOWL HUNTING

A bird which at birth pecks its way out of an egg in northern Canada, and about six months later crosses the Mexican border, presents management problems entirely different from stay-at-home pheasant and quail. Consequently, treaties among the United States, Canada and Mexico place the responsibility for protecting waterfowl squarely upon our federal Fish and Wildlife Service. But, in order to keep sportsmen interested in preserving the necessary wetlands, the "Feds" must also allow as much hunting as the birds can stand without cutting into next year's brood stock.

The majority of hunters and interested citizens believe that the U.S. and Canadian governments, when setting regulations, should allow a margin of safety in favor of the ducks. A very vociferous minority, however, annually accuses the U. S. Fish and Wildlife Service of trying to hold down the kill unnecessarily. The duck hunter who loves his sport enough to care will try to get an impartial appraisal of this situation.

Although it is difficult to follow the lives and times of critters that annually cross at least two national and half a dozen state boundaries, several men have been at this for about thirty years. A look at what they already know is in order.

Men like Herbert Stoddard, Paul Errington and Val Lehman, who have practically lived with quail year-round for several years, have shown that Bob White is a very short-lived gentleman. About 8o per cent of the August quail on your favorite farm will not live until the next nesting season. Their home range is less than a square mile, and if hunters don't bag over half of them, then predators, diseases, starvation and Old Man Winter will give them the Grim Reaper treatment. You can improve the nesting cover, increase the food supply and provide additional places where quail can loaf and sleep safely. If so, your dogs will lock up on point more often come November because fewer nests will be destroyed, and brood losses will be held to a minimum, which adds up to a bigger fall crop. But it appears that you can't do much to increase the percentage that lives long enough to reproduce. 'Tis the nature of the partridge tribe to live fast and die young.

But with most ducks and geese, the opposite is true. One reason may be that the highly mobile waterfowl can spend the winter where food and climate make for easy living. No one knows exactly why ducks live longer than quail and pheasants, or why geese live longer than ducks. But the great backlog of information which has come out of the last thirty years of banding records shows that if they are not shot, Old Greenhead Mallard and Susie will make it up and down the flyway for several years. Every year you read of a hunter getting a mallard, pintail or honker that was banded a dozen years or more previously.

It is true that, year in and year out, about half the adult ducks and 6o per cent of the

Duck banding. Returns from bands reveal much information on ducks to waterfowl biologists. (U. S. FISH & WILDLIFE SERVICE PHOTO BY REX GARY SCHMIDT)

Wooden nesting boxes erected on small ponds and swamps increase the number of nesting sites for wood ducks.

young-of-the-year are making their last trip south. When the season is around seventy days, and the bag limit is four or more, the gun accounts for most of this mortality (bag, plus cripples). Not much of a margin is left for natural deaths from disease and predators.

Fortunately, ducks and geese almost never die of starvation, freeze to death or suffocate in blizzards. About the time the upland game men are digging dead pheasants out of snowbanks in Wisconsin or Colorado, the mallards and pintails are getting fat in the pin-oak bottoms and rice fields of Arkansas, Louisiana or California.

About fifteen years ago Herbert Miller of the Michigan Conservation Department, and a few enthusiastic members of the Michigan United

Conservation Clubs, were trapping ducks on the Detroit River. Using X-rays, they were looking for swallowed shot in the gizzard. We've since learned that we lose about 280,000 ducks and geese in the Mississippi flyway every year, and it may be as bad in other flyways. But in those days, waterfowl managers were just beginning to get some idea of how many ducks die from swallowing shot. While looking for lead in the gizzard, they noticed that about 30 per cent of the ducks were carrying shot in various muscles; it had come not down the gullet, but through their hides! An occasional broken leg bone that had mended, and even a wing bone now and then, showed up in the pictures. Since then, ducks have been X-rayed in several states and

Interior of wooden nesting box showing hen woody sitting on clutch of eggs.

Metal nesting box designed to keep such predators as raccoons from entering and destroying nest. This one is at Remington Farms, Md.

in Canada. In most samples, at least 30 per cent of the ducks going north in spring are carrying shot from wounds received the previous fall.

Band one thousand mallards in Canada and you can expect about two hundred bands from them to be sent in that fall. But several investigators have shown that hunters only report about half the bands they find on their ducks. Otherwise, about four hundred of your original thousand would be reported. Add to that a sizable crippling loss, and you can see that with a seventy-day season and a limit of four or more, we are knocking off about half the southbound flight of popular species such as mallards.

From time to time in the past twenty years the season has been closed on various species

such as wood ducks, canvasbacks and redheads. When the season is reopened, following a year or more of complete protection, the number of ducks shot wearing bands that have been on for two or more years goes up significantly.

This shows that during years of closed seasons, a duck's chances of living to a ripe old age are improved considerably. On the other hand, you can close the ruffed grouse season or the quail season for several years on one area, and shoot the hell out of them on a similar area next door. At the end of ten years you will find the populations about the same on both areas, because natural forces were getting them on one area while hunters reaped the harvest on the other.

But, getting back to ducks and geese, if you

Another artificial duck nesting device at Remington Farms. The metal barrier below is to keep coons from climbing the pole.

Typical biologist's field headquarters. This man is checking age and stomach contents of both pheasants and ruddy ducks.

don't shoot 'em in the fall, they have an excellent chance of living long enough to breed next year and the year after. If they make it through the gunning season, about 80 per cent of the mallards, for example, will overwinter safely and make it back up to the nesting grounds.

As of now, there's not much evidence that more than 5 per cent of them die during the summer months. It all adds up to the fact that next year we'll probably get another crack at the ducks we don't shoot this fall. But a grouse manager or a quail manager cannot say that about his critters. In other words, you can stockpile your duck breeders by tightening up on the season and bag limit, but you can't do that with pheasants, grouse or bobwhites. In setting regu-

lations, the "Feds" have to take this into consideration.

Of course, ducks and water are inseparable, and if we run out of suitable water areas, we will run out of ducks whether we hunt them or not. We must remember that our flat-faced friends are rather specialized in their requirements. Just any water area is not duck habitat. A reservoir too deep for bulrushes and cattails is of no value to canvasbacks and redheads, which nest only in clumps of vegetation surrounded by water. Water that is too muddy for sago pondweed is good for nothing much except as a loafing spot. The effects of oily or other polluted water on ducks and geese are only too well

Every summer ducks are caught wholesale in nets and banded while still on the nest grounds—with such equipment as the airboat in background. U.S. and Canadian waterfowl biologists cooperate—in this case at Johnson Lake, Saskatchewan. (U. S. FISH & WILDLIFE SERVICE PHOTO BY REX GARY SCHMIDT)

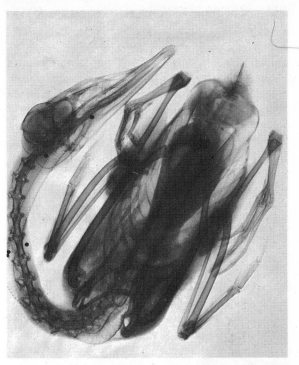

Actual X-ray photos like this one show great incidence of pellets in a wild duck's body. Some pellets come from shooting; others from feeding in places where shooting has been heavy. Latter causes "lead poisoning."

known throughout the country. Water from coal strip mines is particularly deadly.

There are millions of acres of land which are too wet to support a man but not wet enough to raise a brood of ducks, in our northern states and Canada. In northern Minnesota alone, there are about five million acres of tax-forfeited wetland. Elsewhere in the United States are vast swamp forests that are either too far south of the present breeding range, or are unattractive because of lack of suitable water and vegetation.

The very finest duck-nesting habitat lies in the prairie regions of our north-central states and the provinces of Alberta, Saskatchewan and Manitoba. There, except in times of drought, water

and vegetation are made to order. Most of the sloughs and potholes in states such as Iowa and Minnesota have already been drained. The U. S. Department of Agriculture is still encouraging some drainage, in spite of huge agricultural surpluses and efforts by the Fish and Wildlife Service to preserve these valuable wetlands. This is slowing down, and may come to a halt if hunters keep reminding the Department of Agriculture that we have, by their own admission, about fifty million acres now producing surplus crops that could be better used for recreation.

Northern Minnesota, Michigan and Wisconsin have fine examples of wetlands that are boggy but of low value as duck producers. These states are working toward some practical means of opening up these bogs which Nature has filled in over the centuries. If given encouragement and money, they are certain to develop the tools and know-how. In their case, it is primarily an engineering job. If we don't soon convert these areas into good duck habitat, some ridiculous drainage scheme is very apt to ruin their potential.

In the northeast, New York has worked for several years developing small wetland areas, and trying to get breeding stock established by using wild-trapped captive birds. As the human population explosion brings more and more people into competition with ducks for elbow room, such efforts, though costly, will become a necessity.

In Maine, Nova Scotia and New Brunswick, fishing, camping and boating reduce duck production in the marshes where ducks and people occur at the same time. But as Howard Mendell of the University of Maine points out, the vast majority of inland waters in this region, although fine for recreation, are not suitable for nesting ducks. The few marshy areas where nesting blacks and ringnecks occur should be set aside for the ducks. The public will go along with this type of zoning if the need is properly explained.

Down in Maryland, at the Patuxent Research Refuge, Dr. Francis Uhler, of the Fish and Wildlife Service, has been working for years on the conversion of swamp forests into marshlands. In their present state, these have little value as timber, and no value to ducks. He has accumulated a great store of practical knowledge and experience that could have widespread application throughout the southeast. On these new areas Dr. Uhler has also established breeding gadwalls and other species of ducks which formerly did not nest in that region. This is the sort of job that must be done if wetlands which are not producing ducks today are to offset tomorrow's losses of northern marshes.

In the south end of the Mississippi flyway, the vast marshes of Louisiana and Arkansas are maintained by federal, state and private landholders. All three must be encouraged to keep their marshes in usable shape, so that, in addition to their fabulous duck shooting, they will provide enough food and protection to send an adequate breeding stock back north every spring.

Some species, such as the blue goose or the redhead, may be so concentrated at times that a small section of the wintering grounds may hold most of the entire flyway population. In such cases it is always difficult for the local hunters to believe that a shortage of waterfowl can possibly exist. Good management, however, must be based on the entire flyway, for the entire year—including the wintering, nesting, and spring and fall migration seasons, as well as the hunting.

West of the Missouri River in South Dakota, Ingalf Bue and Lytle Blankenship studied manmade stockponds. They found them to be just as productive of ducks per acre as the natural potholes of the Coteau Hills country. But on a square-mile basis they do not begin to compare, because there may be only one or two ponds compared to twenty-five to a hundred natural potholes per square mile.

With the millions now going into subsidized agriculture, and with congressmen casting about for some way to give away money without piling surplus wheat ever higher—well, Mr. Duckhunter, what are you and your buddies in hip boots waiting for? Subsidized stockponds could prove beneficial to ranching as well as ducks, and would not produce more grain for the bursting storage bins.

In Canada the first planned approach to waterfowl acquisition since the Bird Sanctuaries were established in 1925 is offered by the Agricultural Rehabilitation and Development Act. This federal act aims to take submarginal land out of grain production, and improve the farmer's income by encouraging him to use such land to produce the crop for which it is best suited, be it hay, beef, timber or ducks.

Both the Department of Northern Affairs and the Department of Agriculture realize that most waterfowl-production habitat is privately owned. Those potholes built by ancient glaciers are a nuisance to the farmer. Furthermore, they produce ducks which can ravage his crops. If we expect him to leave them alone, we must be realistic enough to pay him for it. Otherwise, we should forget about duck hunting and have a go at blackbirds.

How to get the money from the sportsman who uses the ducks, to the farmer on whose land they are produced is a problem. ARDA could be a vehicle for payment, although it could not, and should not, supply all the money, since the greatest harvest of the waterfowl crop still occurs south of the Canadian border. Canada does, however, take a greater share than most people realize. Could not Ducks Unlimited do some legwork here? Or Wetlands for Wildlife? Or the Audubon Society?

Duck hunters and agriculturists alike must accept the fact that waterfowl production is but one of many uses of the land. Not until the landowner can consider ducklings a legitimate cash crop can we expect him to stop converting his wetlands into dryland crops. It is unreasonable to ask him to produce a crop, for someone else's pleasure, on which he loses money.

Nor should the international boundary be considered a barrier to expenditure of U.S. government funds. Before the duck hunters of North America lose control of additional vital production areas in Canada, we should remember the U.S. government purchases or leases land *in these same areas* for military bases, radar stations, etc. Why not purchase or lease wetlands for waterfowl in Canada?

Although federal and state government programs are an absolute necessity in the United States, Canada and Mexico, many an individual duck hunter has not been content to sit back and hope the government can provide a social-security number and old-age pensions for ducks. In California, for example, the Grasslands Water District, of which J. Martin Winton is president, is a model of cooperation between duck hunters, private landowners, the California Fish and Game Department and the various federal bureaus which deal with water, land and wildlife.

They showed that irrigation water can also be used to produce waterfowl hunting, nesting and wintering habitat. Similar opportunities exist throughout the Pacific flyway. However, instead of the usual excise tax on profit-making bowling alleys, golf clubs and athletic clubs, the public should see to it that hunting clubs which contribute to a natural resource belonging to all the people get a tax break. Lands devoted to reforestation have long received such favored treatment, which is as it should be. Wildlife conservation, along with reforestation, is a public service and should be promoted rather than penalized.

At what is now Remington Farms, on the eastern shore of Cheaspeake Bay, Glenn L. Martin undertook to raise mallards artificially some years ago. Although his mass-production techniques did not contribute significantly to the migratory population, the Remington Arms Company, under the able direction of Dr. Joseph Linduska and Dr. George Burger, took up where the late airplane manufacturer left off. They are systematically working toward production of free-flying, wild-acting mallards. Their scientific approach is in sharp contrast to the short-cuts attempted by most sportsmen's clubs, which invariably wind up with flocks of useless barnyard fowl. Research to counteract predation and promote plants of benefit to waterfowl is also in progress at Remington Farms.

Kenneth Sather, duck hunter from Round Lake, Minnesota, has sponsored a waterfowl research station in cooperation with the University of Minnesota, Minnesota Conservation Department, and the U. S. Fish and Wildlife Service. Mr. Sather's research program is an outgrowth of his hobby of raising ducks and geese from all over the world. By donating pairs of Canada geese to farmers with marshlands, he effectively forestalls their drainage. Says Mr. Sather with a sly grin, "Once the farmer's wife and kids get interested in a brood of goslings, the pothole is not about to be drained."

James Thompson, president of a land-management company in Windom, Minnesota, has succeeded in getting duck hunters to lease potholes directly from the farmers and thus ensure their continued production of waterfowl.

Max McGraw, of Chicago, on his Fin and Feather Farm, has been trying to develop good migratory stock through artificial restocking for several years.

Perhaps the best-known, and certainly one of the most productive, of all private contributions to waterfowl management is that of James Bell, who started with a hatchery on his marsh in Manitoba in hopes of producing wild ducks. He soon realized that this approach would not pay off, so in cooperation with the University of Wisconsin, and Dr. Miles Pirnie, who was then director of the W. K. Kellogg Bird Sanctuary, he established the Delta Waterfowl Research Station. Dr. Albert Hochbaum became director of the Station, and has remained for over twenty-

five years. Much of the great backlog of information on which modern waterfowl management is based was derived from studies performed by this Station. It is now administered by a privately endowed foundation, the Wildlife Management Institute, Washington, D.C.

The famous old Winous Point Club on Lake Erie hired biologist John "Frosty" Anderson, back in 1946. Says Frosty, "My bosses were intelligent enough to listen when I told them I could find out what kinds and how much vegetation they had in the marsh, but as to what each plant meant in terms of food, nesting and brood-rearing cover, we would have to ask the ducks, because this information was not in any book, nor was it known to any hunter, punter or biologist."

Impressed by the results and application of Anderson's studies, the Winous Point Club established its own waterfowl research program in cooperation with the North American Wildlife Foundation, the Ohio State University, and the Ohio Department of Natural Resources.

Fortunately, an intensive summer survey of all birds occurring at the Winous Point marsh was made and published in 1870. The survey was duplicated in 1930 by two members of the American Ornithologist's Union. The number and kinds of nesting waterfowl on the marsh today exceed those of 1870 and 1930 by a wide margin. Although, like all marshes in that region, the annual production does not equal the annual kill, the Club has reason to hope that continued intensive management can eventually bring this about.

At Nilo Farms in Illinois, the Winchester Company has pioneered in developing a commercial duck-hunting preserve system which provides good sport, and reduces pressure on the flyway population. Nilo Farms, under Dr. Edward Kozicky and Mr. John Madson, has also done an admirable job of conservation-education. Their sound, colored movie on the life history of the mallard, done in cooperation with the Missouri Conservation Department, is a classic.

Space does not permit several other examples of private initiative which have made great contributions to the continental waterfowl population and the future of wildfowling. Ducks Unlimited, Wetlands for Wildlife, the National Audubon Society, and Nature Conservancy have all helped preserve important segments of waterfowl living space, and all are worthy of support by every duck hunter.

The research efforts mentioned above have indirectly meant more ducks in front of the gun. Tremendous unsolved problems remain, however, and the crushing pressure of civilization demands a solution as of yesterday. Lead poisoning, for example, knocks off about a quarter of a million mallards annually in the Mississippi flyway alone. Are we to believe that a nation which can put a man on the moon cannot develop a shot which will kill a duck but not poison him if he swallows it? Winchester has a steel substitute which they could probably market if encouraged to do so. Look at it this way: If lead poisoning· could be stamped out, the annual saving in ducks would roughly equal the production on six or seven thousand square miles of fine breeding habitat! It would be so easy for duck hunters to demand—or for the "Feds" to require through legislation—that non-poisonous shot be used by all duck and goose hunters.

The same is true of botulism, or poisoning by

Remarkable set of photos shows how cannon-net trap is used to capture Canada geese for banding in Colorado. A shotgun shell, discharged by radio, propels the net. Once netted, the geese (and ducks) become docile. The birds are banded with metal tags and released to join the main flock. (COLORADO GAME & FISH DEPT. PHOTOS BY GEORGE D. ANDREWS)

blue-green algae, or blood parasites, any of which may kill as many ducks annually as are produced in Montana or Colorado. Just one major breakthrough by research on any of these diseases could mean the difference between a bag limit of four and eight.

The research biologist, whether long-haired, crew-cut or bearded, must stay out in front of the entire management effort at least as far as a man should lead a teal. To let the "Feds" or your own game department falter in this respect is the same as catching a honker in the after end with the edge of your pattern—you watch him lose altitude and drop out of sight, a noble effort wasted.

The subject of law enforcement is all too often left entirely up to the federal game wardens, scattered few and far between across the continent. Frequently, the state game wardens vigorously protect their home county's pheasants, rabbits and deer. But they turn their backs on the marshes full of birds migrating to another state. In fact, there are cases on record where state game wardens were apprehended in waterfowl violations. A few states, however, do not fit this pattern. But why should we tolerate it anywhere? After all, a duck or goose which runs the gauntlet this season has about a three-to-one chance of coming your way again next fall. Can you, then, ignore the pretense at waterfowl law enforcement that exists in many states? Is your state one of those which actually instructs its wardens to stay out of the marshes? A look at the number of ducks confiscated by federal agents that were illegally killed and sold by bootleg rings across the country in very recent years should have opened many a shooter's eye!

The game warden is your ally or your enemy, depending upon whether you are a hunter or a game-hog. If he is your ally, then he should expect, and get, your closest cooperation.

When the drought hit the prairies in the late fifties and left a sizable portion of our nesting ducks high and dry, the "Feds" tightened up on the regulations. Then we began to hear a lot about "species management." Actually, special regulations for various species were in use before the Migratory Bird Treaty Act of 1916. Not until 1961, however, did the full possibilities of this type of management get a long, hard look.

Many duck hunters complain that the fun is gone out of hunting when they have to worry whether their target is a mallard or a widgeon. But species management is here to stay. As the number of hunters goes up, and the supply of ducks and geese goes down, not only the different species, but different areas within the flyways will be subject to special regulation.

For example, in the Mississippi flyway, most mallards don't winter south of Arkansas. In poor mallard years, Arkansas may feel the pinch, while southwestern Louisiana may be up to its ears in scaup. There is no reason why the blue-bill shooter in Louisiana should have his bag limit tied to the upstream mallard population. When widgeon are spilling out over the lettuce fields in California, the duck hunter in the Golden Bear State expects and gets a "bonus bag" of widgeon, even though canvasbacks are completely protected.

Goose hunters at Horicon, Wisconsin, are willing to quit shooting for the year when the quota for the area has been killed, even though the season is in full swing at Swan Lake, Missouri, or Horseshoe Lake, Illinois, where the "goose-kill quota" may be higher.

The hunter who would rather give up his sport than learn the difference between a mallard and a pintail may have to do just that, while the sharper lads will cash in on those species that are riding high while others are in bad shape. With all the excellent museums, movies and books on duck identification, plus your friends who can identify them, there is no need to miss out on the extra fun that comes from knowing your ducks.

In summary, we must elect legislators who are interested in conservation, who will, therefore, allow the Fish and Wildlife Service to apply what is already known in waterfowl management. We must preserve as much as possible of the existing marshland by federal, state and private effort. We must create new habitat by converting bogs and swamp forests into marshes wherever feasible. We must restore marshes that have been drained and abandoned. The research men need our support in fighting disease and lead poisoning, and in gathering the vast quantities of data that are the foundation of regulations. We must sharpen our identification of ducks as well as our aim, to take advantage of species management and reduce cripples. We must give the game warden who is working for us all the help he needs.

These are some of the channels that lead to waterfowl abundance. The duck hunter must travel them all, and travel in the same boat with Canada and Mexico, with private, state and federal wildlife agencies. These are rocky channels, at best, but they are open.

Appendix

How to Shoot a Shotgun

A. Hold the gun by the fore-end with the muzzle pointed UP and AWAY from people, animals and other close objects.

B. Open the action and make certain that there are no loaded rounds in the chamber (rear end of barrel) or magazine and no obstructions in the barrel such as dirt, cleaning rags, grease or ice.

C. Now, close the action gently but firmly. Slamming the action shut causes unnecessary wear.

D. Do not snap the hammer. This is a bad and very dangerous habit to cultivate.

E. Never point a gun at anyone or anything you do not intend to shoot. If you wish to aim at something, choose a distant object (over one hundred yards) and not in line with any person or object.

F. In handling a gun, never swing the barrel end past anyone. Always raise the barrel or lower it before swinging. Keeping the gun pointed up is best. If you should accidentally fire while pointed down, you could hit someone in the leg.

G. When putting the gun away, observe the inspection steps in A, B and C. Always stand the gun in the gun rack, hang it up or lay it down. Never stand it against a wall, automobile, etc., as it is apt to fall down. Many good guns are put out of commission by such carelessness.

H. Always use the proper ammunition in your gun. Don't try a ten-gauge 3½-inch shell in a 2⅞-inch chamber, for example. Never carry a twenty-gauge shell with you when shooting twelve-gauge. You may mix them and end up with a twelve-gauge shell behind a twenty in the chamber. The result usually is a burst gun and injury.

How to Practice at Home

(These instructions are written for right-shoulder shooters. Just reverse them for left-shoulder shooters.)

1. The right-hand shooter should stand with his left foot advanced and pointed a little to the right of the target. Place the right foot about twelve inches to the rear of the left foot and pointing ten to twenty degrees farther to the right.

2. Stand in a normal, semi-relaxed position, leaning forward slightly. Keep your eyes on the target. As you lean in to the target, push the gun away from you in line with the shot. Push the gun out far enough so you will not catch the butt on your clothing as you bring the gun up.

3. Raise the gun so that your right eye (both eyes open) is looking down the barrel at the target. The comb of your stock should be resting gently against the cheek. The butt plate should be about two inches in front of your shoulder. Raise the right elbow slightly to form a pocket and move the gun back so the butt rests firmly on the shoulder. Too much pressure against the shoulder will cause bruising when the gun is fired. If you lean in to the shot and keep your head down, your

eye should be right in line with both the barrel and the bird as the butt meets your shoulder.

4. The gun should be held firmly in both hands, so that some of the recoil can be absorbed by both the hands and arms. The left hand, which is used to steady the gun, should be placed on the fore-end at a comfortable distance from the shoulder. Placing it too far out will cause a slow swing and fatigue. Placing it too close results in a fast but unsteady swing.

5. The head, arms and shoulders should always move smoothly as a unit with the gun. If you follow this pattern consistently, your eyes will always be looking where the gun will shoot. This may appear to be a complicated method of learning to shoot a shotgun, but it is fundamental. Once you get the knack of it, you will run through this pattern automatically. Practice this routine often. When you think you have mastered the technique, try this: Stand about six feet from a mirror and, using your reflected right eye as the target, throw the gun to your face, then to your shoulder. (Never, the face to the gun.) Shut both eyes while the gun is coming up and open your eyes when the butt plate touches your shoulder. If you are consistently putting the line of sight in a four-inch circle, centered on your eye, you are ready to start shooting.

How to Shoot in the Field

If you have mastered the foregoing technique, it will be an easy matter for you to hit a moving target. We believe the following to be a good guide for most people.

1. Determine the direction in which your target is moving.

2. Mount your gun and swing the gun in the direction in which your target is moving. Keeping your eyes on the target, overtake it with your swing, get ahead of it and fire. We recommend coming up from behind and passing on through to get the proper lead. (Imagine your bird is leaving a smoke trail and you are following the smoke to, through and beyond the bird.)

3. Keep your eyes wide open. You will learn to lead correctly, a whole lot faster, if you can see what you are doing when you pull that trigger.

About the only thing that can help you develop correct leading, is practice. There are, however, a few basic facts that will help you establish lead: Remember, you are pointing a shotgun, not *aiming* it. This is due to the speed necessary to shoot a bird on the wing and the spread of your shot. A twelve-gauge full-choke shotgun has a killing pattern of about three-quarters of an inch at the barrel. This becomes seven and a half inches at ten yards, fifteen inches at twenty yards, and has expanded to thirty inches at forty yards. When shooting, you have a fraction of a second to determine range, overtake your target on the swing and fire. You don't have time to aim.

Always estimate your lead from the front edge of the bird. Don't get into the habit of leading from the middle, since some birds are half tail feathers.

The speed with which you overtake your target affects your lead. There are three general ways of pointing out the target, although there are many degrees of difference and variation between each method.

First: Swing and overtake very rapidly (snap shooting). Very little lead is noticeable because the gun muzzle is traveling so fast. The shooter starts to pull the trigger as he is passing through the target relying on the lapsed time between the mental command to fire and the shot leaving the barrel, to establish the required lead. This system is extremely difficult and not recommended for beginners.

Second: Overtake the target, apply your calculated lead (slowing, but not stopping, your swing so that the muzzle is keeping the proper lead distance ahead of the target) and fire as soon as the lead has been determined. This sustained lead is known as "pointing 'em out" and is highly recommended for young and old alike.

Third: Swing way past target, stop and pull

trigger, allowing the target to catch up while you're pulling the trigger. This is guaranteed to make a Very Poor shot out of you. Never Stop Your Swing at Any Time—*Always Follow Through.*

A shotgun trigger is pulled, not squeezed or jerked. You must have perfect timing without pulling the gun off its intended line of travel. In shotgun shooting, the hold is approximate. Because of the large killing pattern and fast movement, the timing of the shot is more important than the exact pinpointing of your aim.

As mentioned above, the speed of the target affects the amount of lead. A rule of thumb which may help you to get your lead is listed below. This is assuming a ninety-degree cross shot, and leads may be cut in half for forty-five degrees, etc.

1. A duck flying against a strong head wind takes a small lead (half a pattern width).

2. A duck flying in quiet air (no wind) takes a lead from four to five and a half pattern widths.

3. A duck which has been shot at, traveling downwind with a good strong wind, takes approximately six to nine pattern widths.

Our last suggestion is this. When in doubt, "get what you think to be the correct lead, double it, and pull the trigger."

Complete Check List of North American Waterfowl

Mute Swan—*Sthenelides olor*
Whistling Swan—*Cygnus columbianus*
Trumpeter Swan—*Cygnus buccinator*
Common Canada Goose—*Branta canadensis canadensis*
Western Canada Goose—*Branta canadensis occidentalis*
Lesser Canada Goose—*Branta canadensis leucopareia*
Richardson's Goose—*Branta canadensis hutchinsi*
Cackling Goose—*Branta canadensis minima*
American Brant—*Branta bernicla hrota*
Black Brant—*Branta nigricans*
Barnacle Goose—*Branta leucopsis*
Emperor Goose—*Philacte canagica*
White-fronted Goose—*Anser albifrons albifrons*
Tule Goose—*Anser albifrons gambelli*
Lesser Snow Goose—*Chen hyperborea hyperborea*
Greater Snow Goose—*Chen hyperborea atlantica*
Blue Goose—*Chen caerulescens*
Ross's Goose—*Chen rossi*
Common Mallard—*Anas platyrhynchos platyrhynchos*

New Mexican Duck—*Anas diazi novimexicana*
Black Duck—*Anas rubripes tristis*
Red-legged Black Duck—*Anas rubripes rubripes*
Florida Duck—*Anas fulvigula fulvigula*
Mottled Duck—*Anas fulvigula maculosa*
Gadwall—*Chaulelasmus streperus*
European Widgeon—*Mareca penelope*
Baldpate—*Mareca americana*
American Pintail—*Dafila acuta tzitzihoa*
European Teal—*Nettion crecca*
Greenwing Teal—*Nettion carolinense*
Bluewing Teal—*Querquedula discors*
Cinnamon Teal—*Querquedula cyanoptera*
Shoveler—*Spatula clypeata*
Wood Duck—*Aix sponsa*
Redhead—*Nyroca americana*
Ringneck Duck—*Nyroca collaris*
Canvasback—*Nyroca valisineria*
Greater Scaup—*Nyroca marila*
Lesser Scaup—*Nyroca affinis*
American Goldeneye—*Glaucionetta clangula americana*
Barrow's Goldeneye—*Glaucionetta islandica*
Bufflehead—*Charitonetta albeola*

Old Squaw—*Clangula hyemalis*

Eastern Harlequin Duck—*Histrionicus histrionicus histrionicus*

Western Harlequin Duck—*Histrionicus histrionicus pacificus*

Labrador Duck (extinct)—*Camptorhynchus labradorius*

Steller's Eider—*Polysticta stelleri*

Northern Eider—*Somateria mollissima borealis*

American Eider—*Somateria mollissima dresseri*

Pacific Eider—*Somateria v-nigra*

King Eider—*Somateria spectabilis*

Spectacled Eider—*Arctonetta fischeri*

Whitewing Scoter—*Melanitta deglandi*

Surf Scoter—*Melanitta perspicillata*

American Scoter—*Oidemia americana*

Hooded Merganser—*Lophodytes cucullatus*

American Merganser—*Mergus merganser americanus*

Red-breasted Merganser—*Mergus serrator*

Ruddy Duck—*Erismatura jamaicensis rubida*

Masked Duck—*Nomonyx dominicus*

Black-bellied Tree Duck—*Dendrocygna autumnalis autumnalis*

Fulvous Tree Duck—*Dendrocygna bicolor helva*

Sora Rail—*Porzana carolina*

Virginia Rail—*Rallus limicola*

King Rail—*Rallus elegans*

Clapper Rail—*Rallus longirostris*

Common Coot—*Fulica americana*

Florida Gallinule—*Gallinula chloropus*

Jacksnipe—*Capella gallinago*

State Conservation Bureaus

(Write these agencies for information on open seasons, lake or stream maps, licenses, hunting regulations, etc.)

Alabama: Division of Game, Fish and Seafoods, Department of Conservation, Montgomery 4

Alaska: Department of Game and Fish, Juneau

Arizona: Game and Fish Commission, Arizona State Bldg., Phoenix

Arkansas: Game and Fish Commission, Little Rock

California: Department of Fish and Game, 722 Capitol Ave., Sacramento 14

Colorado: Game and Fish Commission, 1530 Sherman St., Denver 5

Connecticut: Board of Fisheries and Game, State Office Bldg., Hartford 1

Delaware: Board of Game and Fish Commissioners, Dover

Florida: Game and Fresh Water Commission, Tallahassee

Georgia: Game and Fish Commission, 412 State Capitol, Atlanta 3

Hawaii: Fish and Game Commission, Commissioner of Agriculture and Forestry, Honolulu

Idaho: Department of Fish and Game, Boise

Illinois: Department of Conservation, Springfield

Indiana: Division of Fish and Game, Department of Conservation, 311 West Washington St., Indianapolis

Iowa: State Conservation Commission, East 7th and Court Sts., Des Moines 29

Kansas: Forestry, Fish and Game Commission, Pratt

Kentucky: Department of Fish and Wildlife Resources, Frankfort

Louisiana: State Wildlife and Fisheries Commission, 126 Civil Courts Bldg., New Orleans 16

Maine: Department of Inland Fisheries and Game, State House, Augusta

Maryland: Game and Inland Fisheries Commission, 514 Munsey Bldg., Baltimore 2

Massachusetts: Division of Fisheries and Game, 73 Tremont St., Boston 8

Michigan: Department of Conservation, Lansing 26

Minnesota: Department of Conservation, State Office Bldg., St. Paul 1

Mississippi: Game and Fish Commission, P. O. Box 451, Jackson

Missouri: Conservation Commission, Monroe Bldg., Jefferson City

Montana: Department of Fish and Game, Helena

Nebraska: Game, Forestation and Parks Commission, Lincoln 9

Nevada: Fish and Game Commission, 51 Grove St., Reno

New Hampshire: Fish and Game Department, State House Annex, Concord

New Jersey: Department of Conservation and Economic Development, Division of Fish and Game, 230 West State St., Trenton 7

New Mexico: Department of Game and Fish, Santa Fe

New York: Conservation Department, Albany 7

North Carolina: Wildlife Resources Commission, Raleigh

North Dakota: Game and Fish Department, Capitol Bldg., Bismarck

Ohio: Division of Wildlife, 1500 Dublin Rd., Columbus 12

Oklahoma: Game and Fish Department, State Capitol Bldg., Room 118, Oklahoma City 5

Oregon: State Game Commission, P. O. Box 4136, Portland 8

Pennsylvania: Pennsylvania Game Commission, Harrisburg

Rhode Island: Division of Fish and Game, Department of Agriculture and Conservation, State House, Providence 2

South Carolina: Wildlife Resources Commission, Columbia

South Dakota: Department of Game, Fish and Parks, Pierre

Tennessee: Game and Fish Commission, Cordell Hull Bldg., Sixth Ave. N., Nashville 3

Texas: Game and Fish Commission, Austin

Utah: Fish and Game Commission, 1596 West North Temple, Salt Lake City 16

Vermont: Fish and Game Service, Montpelier

Virginia: Commission of Game and Inland Fisheries, P. O. Box 1642, Richmond 13

Washington: Department of Game, 509 Fairview Ave. N., Seattle 9

West Virginia: Conservation Commission of West Virginia, Charleston

Wisconsin: Conservation Department, State Office Bldg., Madison 2

Wyoming: Wyoming Game and Fish Commission, Cheyenne

Puerto Rico: Department of Agriculture and Commerce, Division of Fisheries and Wildlife, San Juan

Copies of federal laws and regulations affording protection to migratory birds and certain other species of wildlife may be obtained from the Commissioner of Fish and Wildlife, Department of the Interior, Washington 25, D.C.

Regional directors of the Fish and Wildlife Service having administrative supervision over Service functions in the states indicated:

Region 1 (California, Idaho, Montana, Nevada, Oregon, Washington): 1101 N. E. Lloyd Blvd. (P. O. Box 3737), Portland 14, Ore.

Region 2 (Arizona, Colorado, Kansas, New Mexico, Oklahoma, Texas, Utah, Wyoming): 906 Park Ave., S.W. (P. O. Box 1306), Albuquerque, N.M.

Region 3 (Illinois, Indiana, Iowa, Michigan, Minnesota, Missouri, Ohio, Nebraska, North Dakota, South Dakota, Wisconsin): 1006 West Lake St., Buzza Bldg., Minneapolis 8, Minn.

Region 4 (Alabama, Arkansas, Florida, Georgia, Kentucky, Louisiana, Maryland, Mississippi, North Carolina, South Carolina, Tennessee, Virginia): Peachtree-Seventh Bldg., Atlanta 23, Ga.

Region 5 (Connecticut, Delaware, Maine, Massachusetts, New Hampshire, New Jersey, New York, Pennsylvania, Rhode Island, Vermont, West Virginia): 59 Temple Place, 1105 Blake Bldg., Boston 11, Mass.

Canada

Canada: Chief, Canadian Wildlife Service, Ottawa

Alberta: Fish and Game Commissioner, Department of Lands and Forests, Edmonton

Manitoba: Director of Game and Fisheries Branch, Department of Mines and Natural Resources, Winnipeg

New Brunswick: Chief, Fish and Wildlife Branch, Department of Lands and Mines, Fredericton

Ontario: Fish and Wildlife Division, Department of Lands and Forests, Toronto 2

Province of Quebec: General Superintendent, Department of Game and Fish, Quebec

Saskatchewan: Game Commissioner, Department of Natural Resources, Saskatchewan Resources Bldg., Regina

Mexico

Secretaria de Agricultura y Ganaderia, Director General Forestal y de Caza, Mexico, D.F.